$\mathcal{P}$resented to: _____

$\mathcal{F}$rom: _____

$\mathcal{D}$ate: _____

The Tender Trap

Deborah McCorkell Robertson

The Tender Trap by Deborah McCorkell Robertson

Published by:
Insight Publishing Group
8801 South Yale, Suite 410
Tulsa, OK 74137
918-493-1718

Unless otherwise noted, all Scripture quotations are from the New International Version of the Bible.

Scripture quotations marked KJV are from the King James Version of the Bible.

Scripture quotations marked TLB are from The Living Bible. Copyright © 1971 by Tyndale House Publishers. Used by permission.

Scripture quotations marked JERUSALEM BIBLE are from The Jerusalem Bible. Copyright © 1966 by Darton, Longman & Todd, Ltd., and Doubleday & Company, Inc. Used by permission.

Incidents portrayed in this volume are based on fact. However, some names and details have been changed to protect the privacy of individuals.

International Standard Book Number: 1-930027-02-8
Library of Congress Catalog Number: 99-97660

0123456 VP 7654321
Printed in the United States of America

Dedication

To an awesome, transforming God who chose me before the creation of time to love and serve Him so that I might love and serve others who need to see His face.

And to my precious gift, Felicia Nicole, my joyful conqueror, who filled my life with love and purpose.

Acknowledgments

I would like to express appreciation to the following family and friends who indulged me in the completion of this book.

To Yvonne Nance—my editor, spiritual mentor, and friend who was my constant encourager and best cheerleader throughout this endeavor.

To my dear husband, George—who nurtures and supports all my dreams. Thank you for all you do to bring out the best in me.

To my beautiful daughters—who gave me the quiet time I needed to help others.

To Billye Morris—who gave of her time to read and critique this work so that it might be the best it could be.

To Kimberly Hjelt—who looked at this book when it was but a skeleton and envisioned the finished product. Thank you for sitting with me night after night and teaching me how to see with words.

To Jonathan Page—who shared my vision through the embryonic stage and inspired me to get started.

Contents

CHAPTER 1

The Grand Illusion

*O*ur eyes met across the massive foyer. His stare was relentless. Who is this handsome stranger with the charming smile? Is he looking at me? Should I recognize him? The hotel lobby teemed with people. He could be looking at any one of the dozens of people around me. Dare I chance a glimpse to see if his intentional gaze was for me—or someone else? Three times I glanced his way. His scrutinizing eyes never wavered. He began to unnerve me. But at the same time, something about him piqued my curiosity. His eyes were piercing. He was meticulously groomed, his sandy brown hair drew a sharp contrast to his dark eyes. His confident, persistent demeanor captured my interest.

He stood taller than the other men in the room. He was casually dressed in khaki slacks and a tailored navy blazer. Too casually dressed for this classy, high-dollar event.

Amid the throngs in the posh lobby of the Anatole

Hotel in Dallas, I stood alone. The new tower's last brick was laid just in time for the Republican Convention. It was a perfect setting for the vice presidential luncheon.

I was a novice at political affairs. To tell the truth, politics were never my forte. It seemed much ado about nothing, much like a giant flea market where souvenirs and ridiculous convention paraphernalia were sold. It amazed me that people actually incurred exorbitant expenses merely to be seen at this expensive pep rally. Some were invited, *specifically* to write "the big donation check" to confirm their party loyalties. Rah! Rah! for capitalism.

My friend Bill had invited me to this convention a month ago. Bill was twenty-two years my senior. We had been seeing each other casually for about six months. I'm not quite sure how we got started but Bill's life was full of adventure and surprise, and my social life had come to a major standstill after my last heartbreak. Bill acted more like he was thirty-two than fifty-two. He was very active socially and politically and often needed an escort. So I made great sacrifices to attend wonderful events, eat great food, and be treated like a queen. Hey, it was something to do.

Bill's invitation went something like this, "As you know, Deborah, the Republican Convention in August will be hosted in Dallas."

"Yes," I said, already excited about the idea.

"But I will be a vice-chairman and I'll be busy. Would you like to be my guest at the luncheon for the vice president on Thursday and the breakfast ball on Friday? But keep in mind that I can't always be at your side. In other words, I'll be a lousy escort."

"Should I bring a date?" I asked coyly.

"Not unless he's much older than me," he said laughingly.

"How much of a time commitment are you talking about? I will need to make arrangements with my boss . . . and what about the attire?"

"Those are details we can settle later. Besides, you always look great to me, so just say you'll be there," he said appearing a little uneasy and lacking his usual confidence. I began to wonder why Bill was so edgy about this convention. Usually he was cheerful and confident.

Bill said, "You should come and enjoy yourself. This convention will be an education, and you'll meet interesting people. Socially, it's the best thing going on in Dallas in the month of August."

Bill was right. The weather in Dallas during the month of August is almost unbearable. Midsummer is indisputably the locals' favorite time to head for a cooler climate. The humidity may be great for one's complexion, but it's hard to breathe. You feel as though you are moving in slow motion or wading through water.

I could imagine myself the morning of the breakfast ball, dressed in a full-length gown, made up to perfection, and then stepping out into the August heat. At the magic moment when I'm supposed to be making my grand entrance, I could already feel the mascara rolling down my cheeks like black tears. Then, there's always those beads of sweat that form a transparent mustache on the upper lip. How was I supposed to perform with the charm of Cinderella when I could feel my face melting like butter onto hot toast?

After working through this traumatic visualization, I still had the grit to accept Bill's invitation to the ball. So I replied ever so nonchalantly, "Sure, why not?

The convention will be entertaining if nothing else. But as far as meeting interesting people, I'm not convinced."

"What do you mean?" Bill asked.

"Your definition of an *interesting* person and mine differ greatly. *You* never met an uninteresting person in your life. Remember when we went to New York City? You made close friends with the cab driver just from the ride between the airport to the hotel. By the end of a ten-mile cab ride, you not only knew this complete stranger's family members, but also you knew his heritage and had a complete dossier on his past five-year employment history!" We both laughed at the memory.

"Well, Debi, I just love people. You can learn so much from talking *with* them instead of *about* them."

Momentarily he reminded me more of a preacher than a politician. When Bill talked, he had a tendency to address people as though they were his audience and he was the principal character on stage. He welcomed anyone within a twenty-foot radius to join in his conversation. I'm convinced that Bill felt most comfortable on center stage because it required no in-depth interaction.

Nevertheless, even with a twenty-two year age difference, we enjoyed each other's company. We both enjoyed the finer things in life: expensive champagne, great food, the theater, fun friends, and long walks. We were willing to work hard to get what we wanted out of life. Work was our passion, yet we believed in having fun along the way.

Bill was good *for* me as well as good *to* me. He enjoyed treating me like a queen without making me feel like a "kept" woman. Bill wasn't the sugar-daddy that many took him to be. We were close friends who enjoyed the same things. It wasn't as if we had an intimate relationship—I made sure of that. My heart was still nursing a third-degree burn from my last relationship, so it was easy to keep him at arm's length. And Bill seemed satisfied with that, at least for the time being. We gave each other a lot of space and freedom. We had our independence and a great deal of respect for each other. There were few expectations and even fewer demands.

After all the toads I'd kissed along the way, this stable, non-threatening relationship was just what I needed. An adventure—not a commitment. For the past nine months I'd been wandering through a desert wasteland both emotionally and spiritually. I had no idea where I was going or how to get there. Bill appeared to be just the tonic I needed to cure my ailing heart.

As soon as I discovered Bill was a major player in this upcoming convention I understood his uneasiness. Bill never talked much about himself, his accomplishments, or his possessions. He was an influential and persuasive man with definite political aspirations. He possessed a distinguished and professional air. When he put on a suit, you knew he belonged behind a big desk. He wasn't the richest man in the Dallas area, but he was definitely in the top five.

Before the convention, Bill commented to me, "If my man wins the election, I could be offered a cabinet position."

I suspected Bill's involvement with the convention was a way of paying his dues. He gave a significant amount of time, allegiance, and money. In the political arena, when a person does enough and gives enough, he gets an unspoken "payola"—a favor or an appointed position.

On the opening day of the convention I caught the fever of the crowd. I was intrigued and caught up in the spirit of the activities. I planned to take advantage of the situation and attend as many events as possible. Bill had provided me with passes to everything.

On Thursday as I stood in the grandiose lobby of the Anatole hotel, I felt the excitement and anticipation of the Vice-Presidential luncheon accelerate throughout the crowd. With the doors to the Grand Ballroom still closed, the hotel staff scampered about, leaving signatures of perfection on everything from the silverware to centerpieces for the $1,250-a-plate affair.

Bill would be seated as a guest of honor at the head table right next to the late Minnie Pearl and three seats down from the vice president of the United States. I was to be seated at a table he had purchased for a mere $10,000 for his closest friends and family. When the doors opened, I was to be ushered to the proper table. Bill made it sound easy enough, and I was up for the adventure. But you had to wonder what anyone could serve worth $1,250-a-plate!

While waiting for the doors to open, I drifted through the crowd—they were interesting to watch. Suddenly the "watcher" became the "watchee." There he was again! That flirtatious stranger. I could feel his eyes on me. His smile was warm and beckoning. I looked the other way.

I decided to engage in small talk with anyone to discourage his approach. So I exchanged pleasantries with a couple nearby.

After several moments I found my chit-chat wearing thin. He must have been closer than I thought he was because he jumped in to "liven" up the conversation. Smooth but obvious, he'd accomplished his apparent objective.

I was complimented by his tenacity but annoyed at his persistence. The poor unsuspecting couple, unaware of their role in this cat-and-mouse game, chatted away effortlessly with the nameless stranger. Why was I not surprised when he reached out to shake my hand, addressing me? "Hi, I'm Jim Rebel, from Philadelphia."

"Hello. I'm Deborah, from Dallas." I politely shook his hand and immediately directed my conversation again to the couple. I worked at being vague about questions concerning myself. Yet, every time a question came my way, I felt this intrusive stranger was making mental notes. When asked about my profession, I gave a generic, "I work for a major airline."

"What airline is that?" the woman asked.

"American Airlines," I responded, trying not to notice the wry grin on Mr. Rebel's face.

"And what does your job entail?" the woman asked.

My defensive nature quickly alerted me to move into an offensive position. "I'm responsible for a three-state area, which includes sixty travel agencies that have purchased our reservation system. I teach them about our system as well as sell them on additional features that may enhance their productivity."

And before anyone else could comment, I said, "And what about you, Mr. Rebel? You are a long way from home. What brings you to Dallas?"

"I'm a state representative in Pennsylvania. I'm here to make a show of loyalty," he said with a smile, revealing his very cute dimples.

Mr. Rebel was eager to step into the spotlight. His poetically humble attitude quickly won him "The Most Charming Award" of the evening, at least in the eyes of this innocent young couple. Jim's gregarious personality came as no great revelation. My suspicious mind wondered where he'd left his wife. I'd never thought about politicians as single; I assumed they were all married. It made for a more secure public image, or so I'd heard.

Could he be single? Probably not. However, it would not be the first time I'd been pursued by a married man. I wish I had a dollar for every time I'd heard a man say he was separated from his wife, when the only separation was a temporary geographical one.

I decided to test my theory on this tenacious stranger.

"Mr. Rebel, we would love to meet your wife. Is she here?" I asked innocently.

"Sorry to disappoint you, Mrs. . . . ."

"McCorkell. Deborah McCorkell," I said slyly, not satisfying his clever "Mrs." bait.

"Sorry to disappoint you, but I'm not married. I just haven't found my special someone yet," he replied with that ear-to-ear smile that made me blush.

All of a sudden I felt victimized by a game I didn't want to play. Yet, I was the obvious victor due to my new-found information about his marital status, triumphing in his lack of information about mine. Still, I was embarrassed by my participation.

Where is Bill when I need him! I wondered. *He'd put this young whippersnapper in his place!*

Just then, the doors to the grand ballroom swung open. I breathed a sigh of relief—my comfort zone was reestablished. We all moved slowly toward the ballroom door, all except Mr. Rebel that is.

The couple in our intimate little group turned to Mr. Rebel and asked, "Will you be attending the luncheon?"

"Not this year I'm afraid. The price is a little too steep for me. But I really enjoyed the opportunity to chat with you."

"Good luck to you," they said.

Mr. Rebel reached out to shake their hands as they passed into the room. I tried to sneak by him, but he quickly extended his hand to me. He clasped my hand with both of his, asking, "Will you be on the convention floor later this evening?"

"I'm not sure what my plans are, but it's kind of you to ask," I responded politely. I quickly pulled my hand from his and proceeded into the ballroom. I saw Bill sitting on the huge platform at the end of the head table. His smile soothed my anxieties. He nodded cordially as I walked by to be seated at a front-row table near him.

The service was impeccable, and the food was appetizing, colorful and delicious. The ambiance of the room carried that expected distinguished air. The first-class program proved both informative and entertaining. If I closed my eyes, I could easily have imagined I was sitting in the White House. But Cinderella's playtime was quickly coming to an end. It was almost 2 P.M. and time for a reality check. I needed to hustle back to the office. Even though the sales-and-service position in the automation department allowed me a great deal of flexibility, it was a very responsible position and kept me on my toes.

Thursday afternoon, and I had only a day and a half left to close out this whirlwind week. *A couple of productive hours in the office will help make up the time I spent at the luncheon*, I thought as I shoveled through the messages stacked on my desk. *Not to mention the fact that tomorrow will be another late workday since Bill and I are to attend the convention breakfast ball where Charlton Heston is the honored guest.*

Fortunately, my boss was considerate of my opportunity to attend this prestigious event. He was very interested in politics, so he was agreeable to my time off, with the condition that I fill him in on all the details.

I needed to get down to the business of my travel schedule for the upcoming week. But how could I begin to concentrate on next week with the excitement of the days' events vividly dancing in my mind.

The telephone jarred me back into reality. Picking up the receiver, I thought, *Come on, Cinderella! It's time to get back to work.*

"Hello, this is Deborah. How can I help you?"

"You can help me by clearing your schedule for tonight," demanded a male voice.

For a long time I said nothing. I was trying to focus on the voice. *Who is it?*

"This *is* the Deborah who attended the VP luncheon, isn't it?"

"Yes?"

"This is Jim Rebel. We met briefly before the luncheon today."

Momentarily speechless, I finally managed to ask, "How did you find me?"

"Well, you mentioned you worked for American Airlines, and you said you had something to do with sales. So I called the airlines reservations office and told them I was looking for someone who worked in the sales office in Dallas. They transferred me to the Dallas sales office, and someone there knew you. She also knew you had transferred to marketing automation, so she connected me to your office," he concluded triumphantly.

"That is impossible! This is a major company with more than 12,000 people in Dallas alone. That's..., that's impossible!" I stuttered.

"Are you impressed?"

"I'm shocked!"

"I'd rather you were impressed," he chortled. "I think I would have a better chance of convincing you to go out with me this evening,"

I could see a simple 'No, thank you' would hardly be an appropriate deterrent for such a tenacious young gentleman. "I'm indeed complimented by your persistence, but your call surprises me. So let me explain why and with whom I attended the luncheon." And I explained.

But instead of discouraging him, it only intrigued him all the more.

"So?" he questioned.

"During our brief encounter, you gave me the impression you didn't have to work very hard at anything you ever wanted. I guess I was wrong, since I'm sure it took you less than fifteen minutes to track me down in order to continue our deep and meaningful conversation." I hoped my sarcasm was obvious to him.

"Oh, the bittersweet taste of your flattery! I know you are trying hard not to like me, but I'm not going to make it easy for you. I'm rather charming once you get to know me. Just come to the convention tonight and we'll talk. Please. It'll be fun. I'll make it fun," he said convincingly.

"I really can't. My friend, the gentleman whose guest I was today, is a convention vice chairman. I plan not only to protect, but also, hopefully, enhance his image throughout the convention."

"What's your friend's name?" he asked.

"Bill Noble. Do you know him?" I asked.

"Bill Noble is an old man! What are you doing with him?"

Not giving me an opportunity to respond, he rushed on.

"I'm sorry if I seem disrespectful, but if that's who you're seeing, I insist on continuing my pursuit—not during the convention of course. I'm not stupid or unethical. So when I get back home, I'll call you. OK?"

"OK," I said rather weakly. But I wasn't at all sure I wanted to continue this encounter. Why me? Why this zealous pursuit? *Oh, well! Who knows? Who cares?*

Back to work! After this outlandish episode, how could I possibly plunge into three hours of heavy work? I stared at my computer, hoping for some kind of magical inspiration. At this moment, the computer and I were not even on the same planet, let alone the same wavelength.

My mind continued to drift to the breakfast ball scheduled for tomorrow. *What would it be like? Imagine it! A breakfast ball! Such a magical idea!*

What a crazy affair! I was to be adorned in a full-length sequined ball gown, my hair elegantly coiffured—all by 7 A.M. the next morning! This would not be my regular McDonald's drive-through-breakfast kind of morning.

At five o'clock the next morning, I was awakened by the persistent buzz of the alarm clock. Could I possibly turn into Cinderella before daybreak? Where was my fairy godmother who would make it all happen? Why did my soft regal hairdo behave so much better after dark than it did this morning? I hurriedly put on my jewelry as I raced the clock down to the last possible moment and headed for the ball.

I felt drastically overdressed in my sequined gown as I stepped outside my apartment. As luck would have it, one of my neighbors was sneaking out in his bathrobe to retrieve his morning newspaper. We were both embarrassed, as though we were caught in the wrong place at the wrong time. Good thing the sun wasn't up yet, or he would have been blinded by a kaleidoscope of color with me in those sequins.

My neighbor was still looking inquisitively over his shoulder as I climbed into my T-top Camaro, waved nonchalantly, and sped off into the sunrise. Thank heaven, I didn't have to stop and pump gas that morning!

At the hotel, Bill greeted me with an approving smile. Strangely enough, once we entered the ballroom, I no longer could tell what time of day it was. Suddenly, I looked appropriate for the occasion.

The champagne fountains were flowing and the gowns were dazzling. The twelve-piece orchestra played softly in the background while we mingled. More food was served than I could have eaten in a week.

Then, as we sipped our coffee, we listened to Charlton Heston's fervent environmental presentation. When he finished his speech, I excused myself. The time went by all too quickly. My "play allotment" for today was up. Now, I had to run to the restroom for a quick change.

Taking off my rhinestone jewelry and sequined gown, I pulled the loose curls down, tied my hair back to the businesslike style, donned a two-piece tailored suit with matching pumps, and darted off to a normal business day.

I drove to work, my head spinning at all that had transpired in the last thirty-six hours. The rest of my week would be effortless compared to the last two days. Even housecleaning sounded relaxing. I gladly relinquished my convention badge in exchange for a tranquil and, hopefully, uneventful weekend.

LONG-DISTANCE FRIENDS

Exactly one week after the convention, Jim's phone calls began. His persistence revealed a tenacious personality, which added to his charm. I looked forward to his calls. The fact that we lived so far apart kept him at a safe distance. However, my position with an airline encouraged his pursuit. After weeks of telephone conversations, we became long-distance friends and enjoyed sharing our days with each other.

And after each conversation he would ask, "When are you coming to Philadelphia?"

"What's in Philadelphia?" I would ask in my best sarcastic voice.

"You mean besides me? Well, Philly has so much to offer historically and culturally."

"Like what?"

"Like the world-class Philadelphia Orchestra, opera and ballet companies and outstanding theatrical productions, as well as some of the hottest jazz clubs on the East Coast," he boasted.

"I'm not quite ready to pack my bags."

"OK. Did you know that Philadelphia is one of the oldest cities in the United States? The beginning of American history started right here. But interestingly enough, its population is younger than the national average. The median age of adults in Philadelphia is 33.9 years old. That means 40 percent of the population are between the ages of 25 to 54."

"Where are you getting all this stuff?" I laughed.

"From a local magazine. It also says that we are the best restaurant city in America with museums and galleries to spare."

"OK! OK! I'll come."

"When?" he asked in disbelief.

"Let me look at my schedule, and I'll get back to you."

"Great! I'll call you Thursday, and you can tell me what time your flight arrives."

"Wait! Hold on! I didn't say I was coming this weekend."

"Why not? The leaves are beautiful this fall, and the outdoor concert in Fairmount Park on Saturday night is the last one of the season. We could rent a canoe and drift along listening to the music on the Schuylkill River. Or we could rent bikes and ride by some of the most authentic Early American houses in the nation." He pleaded. His infectious enthusiasm tempted me, and I found myself allured by his bait.

"That sounds awfully energetic," I replied.

"Oh! If you'd rather relax, Fairmount Park sports a great picnic area just across from some fabulous eighteenth century mansions."

"What about our nation's hallowed symbol of freedom, the Liberty Bell? Until today the only outstanding feature I knew about in Philadelphia was the Liberty Bell."

"Well, we can't see everything the first time you come. We'll have to save some things for your *next* visit," he said boldly.

"By any chance did you work for the visitors' bureau before you went into politics?"

"No. But I might have to consider it if I don't get busy campaigning for my next term of office."

"Well, I've got to go, but we'll talk Thursday night."

After I hung up, I began tossing around in my head the prospects of such an escapade. *What would it hurt?* I rationalized. *I didn't have anything going on next weekend anyway. What's wrong with meeting a friend for the weekend?* I did such a good job of talking myself into it that by Thursday night when Jim called, I had convinced myself that I should go—just for the fun of it.

When Jim called, I gave him my flight plans and asked him to make a reservation at a hotel convenient to his home. I gave him a credit card number to confirm a late arrival.

Within days I was bound for an unknown adventure, unaware of the tender trap that awaited my arrival.

THE LONG FLIGHT TO NOWHERE

The seat belt sign flashed on for landing in Philadelphia. I felt a strange lump in my throat and I began to ask myself some serious questions. The first question was this: *What if I don't recognize Jim?* I had seen him only once, and that was weeks ago.

Where am I going and why? If anyone had asked me, I'm sure I would have been embarrassed to answer their questions. This trip had all the makings of a soap opera or a horror movie. As a matter of fact, if someone had described to me this same scenario, I might have labeled the leading lady "The Foolish Thrill Seeker."

I really wasn't desperate for a relationship; I had Bill and plenty of other offers. Yet, this had all the markings of a desperate action. I could only assume the void left by an earlier relationship may have paved the way for this curious trip. For months now I'd been blindly dating faceless people. At this point, my life seemed aimless as if I had jumped out of an airplane and was floating downward, waiting for the parachute to open, unaware of how fast the ground was coming up to destroy me.

The next question I asked myself was even more disheartening. *What if Jim is not at the airport to pick me up? No problem*, I thought. I could take the next flight back home.

Actually, I could embark on my own adventure. I could visit the Liberty Bell and other famous spots in Philly.

The next question I asked myself led to many more questions: *How well do I really know this man? How safe will I be? Who will I call if I don't feel safe anymore?* I began to scare myself. Enough questions! Now I needed some answers.

This man was a public figure with a reputation to uphold. Surely he had to be careful with whom he associated. Certainly there must be an unwritten law of conduct to keep public figures in behavioral check. But what if we were not in public? Would he still be accountable for his character behind closed doors?

Fortunately, my flight landed before I panicked enough to hijack the plane. Jim met me at the gate with a lovely red rose. I felt temporarily relieved. And so the adventure began.

He looked like I remembered him. A little over six feet with sandy-brown hair and fervent dark eyes. Even the way he was dressed, in his white polo shirt and khaki slacks reminded me of the first and only time we met. His manly, well-maintained physique would look good in whatever he wore.

Jim warmly embraced me and whispered, "I'm so glad you decided to come." He took the small bag I had carried on the plane asking, "Did you check any bags?"

Trying to appear nonchalant, I said, "Yes, I'll get the claim check for you."

As we walked toward the baggage area, Jim confessed, "You know, while I stood there waiting for your flight to arrive, I wondered if you really had the courage to come. I have to admit I'm pleasantly surprised."

"I'm surprised that *you're* surprised. You *knew* I wanted to see all the historic sights." I said with a dramatic flare.

"Oh! I didn't know you were also patriotic."

"Well, I'm still from the Show-Me State, and I'd rather see it than be told about it any day."

"Jim's one-man tour company at your service," he said with a sweeping bow.

He claimed my bag and escorted me to his car. It was right in front. Holding the door of his snazzy green sports car, he said, "It's a bit early for dinner. Would you like to see some of the local color before we eat?"

"That sounds great!" I replied.

The air danced with nervous energy as we drove along with gaps of uneasy silence. We pulled into an old-fashioned coffee house quaintly decorated with colorful striped tent awnings. At the door we were immediately confronted with the largest shiny gold espresso machine I'd ever seen. Thank heaven, it gave me something to talk about. I thought it was wonderful, and he thought it was wonderful and... then I needed something else to talk about. Instead, I surreptitiously stared at Jim, attempting to memorize his features. I must admit it was much easier talking to Jim on the telephone where I didn't have the distractions of his attentiveness. Other than our brief encounter at the convention, our so called "relationship" was solely vocal.

"I can't believe you really came," he said.

"*I* can't believe I really came either," I responded, as I felt my vulnerability light flashing, *You have placed yourself at his mercy.* My flashing light was right. I felt very vulnerable.

Jim grinned, as though reading my thoughts.

"What's so amusing?" I asked defensively.

"You look like a scared little girl. It's attractive on you," he said seemingly pleased with himself.

"I'm not scared. I'm just a little uncertain. I don't like uncertainty, it makes me nervous," I replied emphatically.

"Oh, I see. What you are really saying is that you've placed yourself in a situation that you have little control over, and you're not comfortable."

"Maybe," I conceded. "Flying off to meet a man I hardly know is not something I make a habit of."

"What a relief!" he chided. We both laughed. "I know this probably won't help, but I'm not weird or anything. I'll even take you to meet my mom if it will help you relax."

"Oh, you have a mom? I feel better already," I whipped.

"Now there's the quick-witted Deborah I know," he retorted.

The ice was beginning to melt. We drank our coffee and casually chatted about our plans.

I had just gotten comfortable when Jim jumped up, declaring, "It's time to go! We've got places to go and things to see. Are you hungry yet?"

"Oh! Your tour includes food?"

"Well, I couldn't decide whether to take you to dinner or to a hotel to neck for a while," he said with a sly grin.

His risqué wit caught me off guard. My face managed to turn many shades of red before I regained my composure.

"And what did you finally decide?" I asked, faking

an air of confidence.

"Dinner! I thought it was the safest option."

We dined at J. J.'s Grotto Restaurant and Jazz Club. The atmosphere was friendly and relaxing. The Italian cuisine combined with a little jazz music made for a perfect setting. The fact that we weren't tucked away in an intimate setting helped ease my defenses.

Fortunately the time change between Dallas and Philadelphia had worked in my favor. By now fatigue was beginning to set in. So I said, "Jim, can we call it a night before I fall asleep and utterly embarrass you?"

"But the night is young! And you're finally here where I can see you and touch you and..." he awkwardly hesitated.

"*And* what?" I asked, suddenly wide awake.

"Nothing. I was just kidding. Relax. I'm a harmless public servant."

"I guess I prefer your jaunty humor in the safety of daylight," I replied. We gathered our coats and walked outside into the crisp night air. Jim politely tucked me into the car. His charming manners appeared sincere and natural rather than staged. His parents had apparently taught him well.

"I know why you're so tired. You date a senior citizen," he teased.

"Bill's not that old. He's only fifty-two."

"Only fifty-two? And your only...?" He hesitated, waiting for me to fill in the blank.

"As Mae West said, 'I'm old enough to know what I want and young enough to get it!'" I said with a smirk.

Jim laughed, "Do you mind if I use that same line sometime?"

"It's not my line, but I'd be careful to whom you say it. It may be a pretty cocky quote for a public servant's image."

"You're right. Thanks for thinking of my best interests. I can definitely see why Bill wants you at his side. But I still wonder what you see in him."

"Bill's kind, attentive, and fun."

"So is my dog, but I don't take him out to dinner."

While trying not to laugh, I spontaneously reached across the car to hit him for teasing me with such a silly comment. As my hand lightly struck his shoulder, he grabbed my wrist firmly. I felt the car begin to slow down, as Jim's undivided attention riveted on me intensely for a moment. Then his eyes focused back on the road.

Still firmly holding my wrist, he gently pulled me next to him. He gradually released my wrist, slowly placing his arm around my shoulder. We drove on in silence. I said to myself, *I think this man has more than a tour on his mind.*

We drove for what seemed a very long time when finally Jim pulled into a residential driveway. I turned to him and asked, "Why are we stopping here?"

"This is where I live."

"Where's my hotel?"

"What hotel?" he asked.

"I distinctly remember asking you to reserve me a hotel room." I said adamantly. "Did you make my reservation? Or is this just another ploy to watch me squirm."

"I thought you were just kidding," he replied sincerely.

If you can visualize an unsuspecting cat backed into a corner by an oversized dog, you might get a sense of what this moment was like for me. I wasn't quite sure if he was toying with me to provoke a reaction, or if the thrill of the chase was on.

Surprised by my reaction, Jim asked, "What's the matter?"

I specifically asked you to make a hotel reservation for me."

"I heard you say those words, but I took it as a joke."

"What made you think I would sleep with you?" I inquired.

"Certainly you didn't come all this way just for dinner?" he snapped.

"I certainly don't have to fly 2,000 miles to find someone to sleep with," I replied, my voice raising along with my Irish temper. "You may be a master of manipulating public opinion, but I'm not so easily dominated."

My controlling personality wasn't always an asset, but it usually protected me from situations like this one.

Jim sat there in silence for a few moments. Then he said apologetically, "I'm sorry, I made an assumption that I shouldn't have. Please forgive me. I'm sorry if I insulted you, but you must know that was not my intention. I care about you. I want you to be happy with me as well as with the sleeping arrangements.

"It's after two o'clock, and the closest hotel is twenty miles away. If you stay at a hotel, it may be noon until I see you again."

I started to interrupt, but he didn't even take a breath and went on.

"But I'll gladly take you to the hotel if that's what you really want. However, if you decide to stay in my home, you can have my bedroom upstairs. I'll sleep downstairs. Don't worry, I promise to be a perfect gentleman. Trust me!"

"Why should I trust you?" I questioned.

"Did you really travel more than 2,000 miles thinking you couldn't trust me?"

He had made his point. What should I do? Was I really blowing things out of proportion? Or was I falling prey to manipulation. Should I stand on principle and make him drive me the twenty miles back to the closest hotel?

What flaw in my personality made me always consider another person's inconvenience before my own? Could the motivation be fear of never seeing Jim Rebel again? I didn't even know him that well. I can only speculate that it must have been the fear of rejection. I realized that I wasn't ready for rejection by anyone at this specific time in my life. So I gambled. I took Jim at his word. After all, he had his reputation to protect. Right?

"I'm sorry if I offended you. Please try to relax." Raising his right hand he said, "I, Jim Rebel, do solemnly swear not to set one foot upstairs until the sun rises, unless invited of course."

"Fat chance!" I said finally able to laugh.

"However, I do take a shower in the upstairs bathroom every morning. But it's at the other end of the hall," he said as he escorted me up the stairs. I felt like I was being led, emotionally, further and further into a dark maze. The further I walked, the darker it got. Finally, unable to see, I groped in vain for my boundaries. Could he possibly see behind my well-groomed facade to perceive the vulnerable victim I'd become?

My humble prayer that night went something like this:

> Oh, night be quick! Take away my fear, O
> mighty God! Seal this unlocked door, so
> that no harm may come to your foolish
> child.
> O, merciful Father!

May I feel Your grace shining on my face as
the sun rises this morning.

Only five hours after I closed my eyes, the morning
sunshine peered rudely through the window bringing
a new day. All went well through the night. All
promises were kept, and Jim's honor had been
restored in my sight, and my strength was replenished
for a fresh start.

After breakfast we started our tour of Philadelphia,
"the City of Brotherly Love." We began at Independence Square, my favorite historical sight, where the
name, "the United States of America," originated.

Independence Square also included Independence
Hall, where the Declaration of Independence was
signed and written. I stood in the very square where
the Liberty Bell first rang out.

Also at this identical location, Thomas Jefferson,
Benjamin Franklin, and other patriots wrote the famous
words: "When in the course of human events . . .," proclaiming the Declaration of Independence. Here men
looked deeply inside themselves and asked, "What do I
stand for? What would be so important that I would die
for rather than live without?"

Staring at the Constitution, the actual document, I
thought to myself, *I wonder how we managed to reverse
those priorities to read, The pursuit of happiness, personal
liberty—at the expense of human life.* If the order of
these principles worked so well for our forefathers,
why did we think we had the right to alter them?

Accompanied by Jim, my own personal tour guide, I
learned all the inside scoop about the birth of our
nation. I found out that Philadelphia was the home of
the first American hospital, the first American medical
college, and the first women's medical college.

Philly's museums and fabulous art galleries appeared endless, but visiting the historical sights intrigued me the most. This city gave me an overwhelming sense of patriotism. As I reflected on the events that took place on that very ground, it imparted a fresh perspective on life.

Did the original settlers realize the value of their selfless actions? Even though thus far my existence seemed insignificant in the scheme of time, I suddenly craved a purpose in life so that the generations to follow would know I'd been here and had somehow made a difference.

But what purpose could I possibly possess that I would be willing to give up my life for? Had I become so shallow and self-centered that nothing would be worth dying for? This question waged a battle inside me. Was I born only to live life accidentally—to endlessly wander on a path to some unknown destination? I needed to find a purpose. I yearned to know my purpose as well as what I stood for.

Jim interrupted my deep reflection when he asked, "What are you thinking about so hard?"

I opened up my heart and showed him a little bit of the real Deborah.

He just commented, "You'll get over it when the newness of the city wears off."

I didn't want to get over it! I wanted to savor it and grow from it. Somehow, "life, liberty, and the pursuit of happiness," rang in my ears the rest of the day.

When evening fell the second night, Jim came up behind me, gently taking me by the shoulders, whispering, "Since you're leaving tomorrow afternoon, I would love you to spend the night in my home again tonight if possible. That way we can maximize our time together tomorrow. But if that's not acceptable, it's all right. No pressure!"

"Well, if the same conditions apply tonight as last night, I'll stay."

We enjoyed a quiet evening cooking and watching television together.

I awakened the next morning to discover that Jim was a man of his word. And before we headed for the airport, he took me to an elegant hotel for brunch.

We went through the airport routine and finally arrived at the departure gate. We sat there just looking at each other as if to say, "Where do we go from here?" I don't think either of us were prepared to answer that question right now.

I hate good-byes—temporary or permanent—so I wanted to part quickly.

"Thanks for coming," he said awkwardly, as they called my flight to board.

"Thanks for a great tour. I'll have to recommend you to some of my friends," I said as I gathered my things.

He just laughed and shook his head as if to say, "The perfect exit line for the quick-witted Deborah!"

I waved and dashed on board to the safety of my known environment. I fell into my seat exhausted from a marathon weekend and settled back to enjoy the flight.

Now what? I thought as Philly fell behind me.

My impulsive adventures often left me facing the "Now what?" Much like Scarlet O'Hara in *Gone With the Wind*, the phrase I'd used in such cases since childhood fit right here, "Oh, well! I'll think about that tomorrow."

I was thankful to return to my safe, quaint, two-bedroom apartment. After such a risky weekend, I had a new appreciation for the mundane things in life, like laundry, cooking, and cleaning. Doing everyday things had a way of bringing me back to reality. I wanted to stay far away from speculation and the ever dreaded "What if?" questions.

CHAPTER 2

Angel of Mercy

Monday morning my phone rang just minutes before the alarm burst into its rude clamor. "Hey girl, how was your weekend?"said the ever energetic Bill. I don't know what kind of vitamins this man was taking, but I needed some desperately.

"Good morning, Bill."

"Come on, jump out of bed. I've already jogged three miles, showered, and eaten breakfast. Listen, I've got a great proposition for you."

"OK, OK. I'm up. Now speak slowly," I said, still groggy with sleep.

"I've got to go to Hong Kong for a couple of days to finalize some business, and I want you to come along and keep me company."

"When are you leaving?" I asked, wondering if I heard him correctly.

"I'm leaving for New York tomorrow to catch the Concorde out of Kennedy. It's less than four hours to London. I thought we'd go to the theatre and run through Harrod's for a quick shopping spree before we jumped back on the Concorde for a twelve-hour nap to Hong Kong. The whole trip won't take more than five days. So what do you think?"

"Think? I think I'd better call you back after I have a cup of tea. For a minute there I thought you just asked me to fly to the other side of the world with you and leave tomorrow."

"Oh, come on. Do you have a better offer?"

"Are you serious?" I asked.

"Yes, I'm very serious! I promise to be a gentleman. You can even hold on to your return ticket so that if at any time you get bored with me and want to go home, you can. I just don't want to make this trip alone, and besides, we haven't seen each other in a while, and we can catch up with what's going on in each other's lives. What do you say?"

"Bill, what a great offer but . . ."

"No buts. I hate the word 'but.' I never like what comes after it."

"Bill, today I start my six-week marathon training for my new position as a computer specialist."

"Reschedule it," he insisted.

"I wish I could, but there are thirty other people taking the same training class, and it starts today in two hours. It's not that I don't appreciate the offer. I really do. You have to know that I would love to go. What a great experience! But you do realize how important this new position is to me, don't you? Once I have automation and sales training with a company like American, I can get a job anywhere. Please tell me that you understand."

"I understand, but that doesn't diminish my disappointment," he replied.

"I'm sure you won't have to make that offer too many times before you have someone who will jump at the chance," I consoled.

"But you're my best talking buddy, and I love seeing

things through your eyes. You always add life to the mundane events in my life."

"Thanks. I think you're special too. Bill, I've really got to run, or I'll be late. You know how important first impressions are. I'll talk to you after I get through this training."

"Then you'll be busy with your new job. I know how that is. I'll call you in a couple of months and check up on you," he said.

"That will be great. Have a wonderful trip. I hope you find someone special to go with you," I replied as I hung up the phone and ran for the shower. I was really looking forward to this new position with the company, but not the grueling training.

I would spend the next six weeks at the training center. Three other girls and myself would become very intimate as we crammed together in a small living space as we ate, drank, and slept computers. I can only assume our teachers thought that if they kept us constantly in the presence of our computers, talking to them, learning from and about them, eventually we would think like them.

At the end of six weeks, our brains were to equal the size of the largest main-frame computer. We were to become specialist in a mere forty-two days! Little did our public suspect that the only difference between us and the computer ignorant was this whirlwind training course.

In the midst of this organized chaos, mandatory female bonding, and mind-rending burnout, I met Cassie, one of three roommates. Cassie and I discovered we had a lot in common. We were both the type that kept to ourselves. We didn't stay up late to party with our roommates who treated this training session like a six-week juvenile pajama party—junk food, wine and beer, off-color jokes, and incessant chatter—prolonged adolescence.

I have always been a loner. Sometimes I wondered why I enjoyed being alone so much. Maybe it was a result of growing up with eight siblings and *any* moment of silence was golden. Whatever the reason, I enjoyed my own company. This is why I found it unusual to enjoy eating most of my meals with Cassie.

As our friendship grew, Cassie confided in me. One evening as we walked on the training center grounds, Cassie told me about her older sister, Deborah, who had died tragically just a few years before.

"I'm so sorry. How did she die?" I asked.

"She contracted hepatitis from a blood transfusion. It weakened her system and eventually it took her life."

I could sense Cassie's pain as she recalled her sister's death. She confided that Deborah was the favored child, loved by all who knew her, especially Cassie's parents. Deborah's death left deep emotional wounds in Cassie, and from the tone of Cassie's voice, some of these wounds were still fresh. Cassie didn't understand why God had taken Deborah instead of her. She was plagued with the regrettable feeling that she would never be able to measure up to Deborah's beauty, brains, and charm. Cassie felt she could never replace the joy Deborah had brought into her parent's lives.

My heart sincerely went out to Cassie, but I had no idea how to comfort her. All I could provide was a sympathetic ear and genuine friendship.

I saw the pain in Cassie's eyes every time she called me by name. No doubt, my name brought back a flood of painful emotions. I hoped my association with Cassie would somehow assist in her healing process.

One evening as Cassie was telling me about the day

her sister died, she said, "I don't know how I could have survived without the help of my church family. They nurtured and sustained me through the weeks and months of my grieving process."

My ears really perked up, "What did they do?" I asked.

"The many hugs, the constant words of encouragement, and genuine love constantly affirmed me. They sent cards, took me out to lunch, and invited me into their homes. They just loved me."

"Do you go to a small church?"

"Actually, it's a large church, but I belong to a close-knit singles group."

I felt myself wince inwardly at the mention of a singles' group. Too many times I had fallen prey to cleverly concealed meat markets masquerading as singles' groups, even in church. But Cassie seemed so solid, surely this group was different.

"I've been trying to find a church home," I said.

Cassie was such a good listener that I just blurted out all my religious frustrations to date.

I told her that I was raised Catholic, but I couldn't seem to get beyond the rituals and traditions. As a child, I found that kneeling in a dark box with a secret sliding door was not only intimidating but scary. They called it "the confessional." But I always felt there had to be a better, more personal way of approaching God. Confessing my sins in an open field, staring up into the majestic sky seemed more direct and personal.

I confessed to Cassie that I wanted a closer relationship with God. I wanted to talk directly to the God of the universe. I wanted to be able to talk to Him whether I was sitting, kneeling, lying or standing in line for lunch. I wanted to know that God would hear my prayers anytime, anywhere.

I said, "Cassie, there so many things I don't understand about the Catholic Church. I don't understand why I have to make the sign of the Cross to begin every prayer, then again to mark the end of every conversation with God. I'd like to be able to just look up and say, 'Good morning, Father. What's on the agenda. What can I do for You today?'

"I'd like to identify with the Son of God instead of living in fear of Him. I'd like to think that if Jesus walked on earth today, He might wear blue jeans as well as holy robes."

"Cassie, let me rattle on without interrupting," and after a long pause I said, "Sounds crazy, huh!"

"Not really," she said. "But why should you let rituals stand in the way of your relationship with God? A lot of people seem to enjoy rituals and traditions. I suppose it makes them feel bonded to their heritage, much like family holiday traditions. Also, I've heard other Catholics say that the act of going to confession gave them a great sense of relief when they would hear the priest say, 'Your sins are forgiven. Go and sin no more.' I can only imagine that many Catholics received those words as if they were receiving them from God Himself."

"I guess I've come to envision God as the mighty giant in the *Jack in the Bean Stalk*. If I dared exert the physical strength to climb up to His domain, I would be so intimidated by His awesomeness, I'd tremble if He dared glance my way,." I said with a dramatic flare.

"Well," Cassie smiled, "I wish I could reach up and pull God down from the clouds for you, but that's something you'll have to do for yourself. I think you're on the right track though. You just need the Spirit to guide you."

Spirit to guide me! I thought. *Hmmm. That's some-*

thing I'll have to tuck away and ask about later.

"Cassie," I said, almost defiantly, "I cannot be anything but what I am. I just have to believe that God can carve from driftwood as well as from redwood," I said sounding a little philosophical.

"I believe you're absolutely right," she agreed, then said, "Why don't you come to church with me this Sunday? Our church is full of friendly people, and they always welcome guests."

"What kind of church is it?"

"It's called Calvary Temple."

"Is it Jewish?" I asked quickly, thinking of a Jewish temple.

"No! Our church is Assembly of God, but people of many religions attend—even Catholics," she said laughingly.

Cassie's enthusiasm convinced me to give it a try. I accepted cautiously, yet with expectancy in my heart. "I'll come! What time should I meet you?" I asked, thinking, *A compassionate church might be just what I need right now to help me gain some kind of spiritual focus.*

"Meet me Sunday morning at nine o'clock in front of my church, and we'll go in together. I'll call you later with directions," Cassie said as she left training that day.

"I'm looking forward to it! See you then!" We waved and parted. I felt the seed of a lasting friendship had been sown.

The following Sunday I met Cassie outside the church. We rattled on, talking computer lingo for a few moments, rapidly catching up on our jobs and exchanging a few war stories. As we went inside, Cassie made several quick introductions. Once inside the sanctuary, I sensed a warmth I had never experienced before. Happy people with friendly faces filled the room.

Cassie continued to introduce me to many people who appeared honestly glad to meet me, almost as if they'd been expecting me. Positive interchanges left me with the impression that these people were genuinely interested in me. I felt welcomed and special.

Later that evening as I reflected on the day's events, my suspicious mind questioned the kindhearted nature of everyone I met that morning. *Why are these people so happy? Why are they interested in me?* I pondered. My curiosity inspired many more visits. The messages from the pulpit were full of love and compassion, and I kept hearing how much God loves us. Well, that was no great revelation. I had heard that all my life, but I had not experienced the reality of it.

The pastor got my full attention when he said, "God desires a personal relationship with *you*. God desires a relationship with you even before He desires your obedience."

He continued, "Let's look back at God's choice for a king to reign over His people, Israel. King David loved God dearly, but David wasn't always obedient. Yet David's disobedience never separated him from God, because God knew David's heart."

That was it! *God knows my heart!* The tears began to fall as I bowed my head and covered my face. For the first time in my life, I actually missed the kneeling bench in front of the pew so graciously provided by the Catholic church.

But at that moment, it didn't matter what church I attended or at what pew I knelt. What mattered was that I opened my heart to *God*. I would never be good enough to deserve God's love, but the treasure lay in the fact that He didn't expect me to be good enough. He loved me just the way I was.

Finally came these profound words, "Jesus Christ

came to earth, lived as a human, and died on the cross for every sin you ever committed."

I knew that, but what made this age-old message sound so alive today? I felt God's love and compassion flowing from the pastor as well as from those around me. The pastor looked right at me as he explained God's compassionate heart.

He said, "God loves you, not for what you do or don't do. He loves you because He made you. He made *you* just the way you are, and He made you for a specific purpose. You are special to Him."

The entire congregation acted as if they believed every word this pastor said. And I must say, his words were sinking into me like water into a dry sponge. No wonder everyone was smiling. Their thankful faces reflected God's love. It was obvious they *knew* God instead of just *about* Him. People's faces were radiant as they freely lifted their hands toward heaven. How had they come to believe in God's love so wholeheartedly? I needed to know.

I watched intently, trying to discover this mystery. I watched husbands and wives go hand in hand to the altar to pray together.

I saw men put their arms around their wives as they prayed, as if to say, "You are special to me, and I honor you before God."

I couldn't stop the tears from flooding my eyes. Where had these godly men come from?

I returned to church for the evening service. I even attended on Wednesday night. Something inside me continually drew me. I never attended church three times in one week before in my life. And more surprising than that, I couldn't wait to return! Something was happening to me. The lifelong knowledge of God carefully stored in my head began to filter down to my heart. God was changing me, but I needed to know so much more. I felt I was on the verge of finding what my heart had been crying out for.

Cautious, but intrigued I returned time after time to this church. I became involved with the singles class. It was in this class where I met my lifelong and closest friend, Carmen. As it turned out, Carmen also worked for American Airlines, so we shared a mutual interest.

Carmen worked hard to befriend me. Every time I entered the church doors, there she stood with a warm smile and a hug. *She must live here!* I thought. Friendliness is one thing, but she was outright persistent to establish a relationship. Maybe Cassie had told her about me and had asked her to watch out for me. Whatever the case, I wasn't use to such tenacity.

In spite of Carmen's over attentiveness, I liked her. What wasn't to like? She always looked happy to see me and was always trying to make me feel at home. But I was a woman with a mission. I wasn't coming to this church to find friends; I was coming to find God. I had not yet understood that God had already been exposing Himself in every friendly face I met.

Besides, I was still too wary of strangers to allow anyone to get close. They didn't *know* me, so what did they want? I'd learned from many disastrous relationships, from an early age that intimacy leads to hurt and disappointment, so avoid it if at all possible. And if strangers wanted to be close, that meant they wanted something. Why did these Christian strangers want to be my friend? What did they expect to get from me?

One Sunday morning I decided to sleep late. I'd had a long week on the road and decided to relax. But all the while I lay in my bed, my mind kept thinking about the warmth and gracious atmosphere of Cassie's church. I surprised myself when I realized I was actually feeling disappointed and guilty about not making the effort to go.

About noon the phone rang. It was Cassie. "Hey girl, where have you been?"

"I got in late on Friday and decided to lay low this weekend. I've got a crazy week coming up, and next weekend I'm hopping on a flight to Philadelphia to visit a friend."

"That sounds exciting. I've never been to Philadelphia."

"It is exciting, but I'm not so sure I should be going now."

"Why do you say that?" Cassie questioned.

"It's a long story. When I get back, I'll tell you all about it." I wasn't sure Cassie would condone such a trip.

As the weeks passed, I saw little of Cassie due to her traveling schedule. But Carmen gladly stepped in as my spiritual and social chairperson. If I missed going to church even one week, Carmen called to check on me. I had a guardian angel, like it or not.

IT'S NOT WHAT YOU KNOW—IT'S WHO YOU KNOW

How do I learn to love God? I wondered. Why did something that sounded so simple draw such a blank in my mind? I loved God. But did I love Him personally? I decided to find out what love really meant.

According to The American Heritage Dictionary *love* is "an intense affectionate concern for another person. A beloved person. Used as a term of endearment. A strong fondness or enthusiasm for something."

Theology defines love as "God's benevolence and

mercy toward man. Man's devotion to or adoration of God. The benevolence, kindness, or brotherhood that man should rightfully feel towards others."

Did I have an intense, affectionate concern for God? Was I devoted to Him? Did I adore him? My spiritual background told me yes, but my heart confessed that I only knew about him. How could I love someone I only knew about? What was the mystery behind a loving relationship? How could a concept so simple be beyond my comprehension? I don't think the library's definition offered much help with this question.

I needed a sharper shovel to dig deeper than my comfort zone allowed. I had come too far to turn back now. I had to uncover this perplexing enigma.

As I lay in bed one night as questions raced through my head, I slipped out of bed and fell to my knees. I always felt like I interrupted God when I addressed Him directly asking for something. It seemed selfish to bother God with my curiosity when the world was full of people with real problems. But on this night I just had to know. And somehow, "Excuse me" just didn't sound like the right way to begin. So I decided to just be quick.

"God, please reveal the mystery keeping me from an intimate relationship with You. I hear You offer the power to transform lives through a personal relationship with You. My life could sure use a transformation. I've searched all over the world for happiness. All my efforts are falling short of filling the void in my life. I know this is just a little thing, but it would mean a lot to me if You would just tell me how to love You, please."

Not long after that, my Bible reading came alive. Instead of struggling to read and understand it, I read my Bible with the same enthusiasm I gave to the latest hot novel. I read about Jesus' life experiences, ranging from birth to adulthood. He ate, He slept, and He worked with His days full of activity but not anxiety. I knew why Jesus died for us, but I was just now discovering why He lived for us. Jesus lived on earth to show us the love and compassion of the Father. He not only taught us to love and forgive but how to deal with hardship, suffering and injustice. He showed us the way through His words and action. Jesus left some pretty big footprints.

For several weeks I isolated myself from everything but work, church and reading the Bible. Understanding the heart of Jesus as He walked on earth filtered the knowledge of God from my head to my heart. I discovered the key to an intimate relationship with the heavenly Father in the difference between *knowing* Him and *knowing about* Him.

My life became more focused and fulfilled. The aching void once consuming my heart was steadily replaced with love and companionship. Although my spiritual destination remained unclear, at least my internal compass pointed straight up to God.

Reflection on questions like why God loved me and why He sacrificed His only Son increased my eagerness to know more about God. He obviously didn't do it because I loved Him or because I was worth dying for. Love's mystery began to unfold as I reflected on my parent's love for me, which began miraculously at my birth. They loved me because I was part of them.

Suddenly logic set in! My earthly parents loved me because I was bone of their bone and flesh of their flesh. I had their eyes, their features. They saw themselves in me. If my parents loved me just because I came *from* them, how much more could God love me when He *created* everything about me. God had claimed me long ago.

"I will not forget you. See, I have engraved you on the palms of my hands."
—Isaiah 49:15-16

Just as my relationship with my parents developed slowly as we shared each others' joys and sorrows, that is how I could develop my relationship with Jesus. It was a process of getting to know someone's heart. My parent's love also did not hinge on who I would or would not become. Their love did not hinge on my obedience, neither did God's. Wow! The fog was lifting!

Now if I could just get a handle on the concept of God's self-sacrificing love. I wanted to know who could love someone enough to give up His life for any person? Or even more puzzling, who could sacrifice His only child for someone else? I was sorry to say that I couldn't think of one person on earth for whom I was willing to give my life. Maybe the pain and disappointment I'd experienced had hardened my heart, making me unable to relate to that kind of love. Or maybe that kind of love only existed in heaven.

I *could* relate to the Son of God because He came to earth to live as we lived, to love as we loved, to cry as we cried, and to face death as we must face death. It was God the Father that was still a mystery to me. However I was convinced that the secret to knowing God the Father lay in knowing the heart of His Son, so I set out to dip deeper into the heart of Jesus.

DO ALL RELATIONSHIPS HAVE A PURPOSE?

As my relationship with Jesus grew, my life changed. I became confident in my purpose for living. What an awesome feeling to discover why you were created, to no longer live life accidentally and struggle to make life's mammoth decisions! Jesus sent the Holy Spirit to help and guide me in all my decisions. If I listen to the Spirit, I stay on God's course for my life. I figure if God can hang the stars and create the universe, then He can handle keeping my life on track. Besides, since He is the only one who knows what my purpose is, I think it's wise to communicate with the Guy in charge.

My new relationship with Jesus affected the way I viewed all of my relationships. Surely if I were created for a specific purpose, then every other person who touched my life must also have a role in that purpose. So I began to look closely at the people God placed in my life to examine their purpose as it related to me.

As the weeks continued to roll on, so did Jim's long-distance calls. Our conversations were centered around my new found church friends and church activities. Through our conversations, I realized Jim didn't exactly share my excitement for my new church. For the first time I began to question my relationship with Jim. Did he have a purpose in my life? If Jim and I were going to develop a relationship, I wanted it to be a meaningful one. So I began to ask myself some significant questions, such as, Were we compatible? Did we like the same things? What was important to him? Where did he stand spiritually?

I wanted to know so much more about him than I already knew. I wanted to know about his values and his priorities. I wanted to know about his parents, his family, his first girlfriend. What were his long-term goals? What was his biggest disappointment in life, and how did he handle it? I wanted to know his favorite foods and how he liked to spend his time.

I carefully planned my next trip to Philadelphia with a new found purpose. Content with the understanding that this latest jaunt had a definite agenda, I was much more relaxed when Jim and I made plans for our next weekend together. I couldn't wait to learn all about his life.

When I arrived in Philly two weeks later, I was relieved to see Jim standing at the gate. His face lit up with a warm smile as he handed me a single red rose. We quickly gave each other a cordial hug and headed toward the baggage-claim area.

My state of mind possessed a new confidence. My purpose gave me a defined direction instead of moving with an impulsive whim. My "que sera sera" attitude had burgeoned into a mission of fact finding.

"Are you hungry?" he asked, as we collected my baggage and headed to the parking lot.

"As long as we're not eating airline food," I responded.

"Great! I've got a perfect place picked out for lunch. Even if you're not hungry now, you will be when you smell the aroma of fresh-baked bread coming from the kitchen of this restaurant."

A restaurant is a great place to talk and open up, I reasoned. This will fit ideally into my plan, I schemed. At first I thought it best not to be too obvious about my specific goals for this trip. He may get a little suspicious if I started playing a game of twenty questions too soon. Patience would be imperative for implementing my plan. However, patience was not a character trait I possessed. I wanted to know everything about Jim, and I wanted to know it now! I didn't want to waste my time flying back and forth to Philadelphia if this guy wasn't for me. My controlling personality demanded a plan—a definite direction. My strategy prevented me from getting caught off guard and upsetting my confident but fragile facade.

Jim parked his snazzy sports car in front of the Caribou Cafe, a restaurant in an elite part of town.

"Do you like French food?" he asked, as we entered the chic restaurant decorated in a country French motif.

"I love French food. I could sit for hours in a place like this."

"This is Philadelphia's first authentic French cafe," he explained.

Jim chose a quaint table on the outdoor patio. The weather was perfect, just cold enough to wear a warm wool sweater, but chilly enough to smell hints of winter.

As soon as we ordered our lunch, I couldn't seem to help myself. I had to get on with the business at hand—my quest to "know" Jim.

"Tell me about your parents, Jim. Do they live here?" I asked attempting to act casual.

"They live about twenty miles from me. They're pretty average folks. My dad is about to retire, and my mom is a good cook." he responded. His information was a bit scant for my tastes, so I queried further.

"What business is your dad in?" I continued.

"He's a mechanical engineer. Not a very exciting job, but he has always loved it."

"What do your parents think about your being a politician?"

"To tell you the truth, I've never asked them what they think, and they've never asked. They're pretty wrapped up in my sister's life right now. She has two young kids, and Mom and Dad love being grandparents. I think my marital status is more important to them than anything I might do as a profession," he said thoughtfully.

Just then our lunch was served. I opted to give this family investigation a rest. After all, I had plenty of other topics to cover.

After lunch we drove along the Schuylkill River that divides the central city from west Philadelphia. After driving for an hour, we had covered only a small portion of Philly's 130-square mile historical metropolis. Jim was once again a gracious guide, pointing out the historical significance of each notable building and monument. What better way to see a historical city than through the eyes of someone who served it. But I could sense Jim's eagerness to move on to *his* agenda.

Within a short time, we left the city and headed to the small county outside Philly were Jim lived. Our twenty-mile drive was picturesque and spectacular. As we traveled, the sights presented a melodious contradiction of visual imagery. The earth's natural beauty left its autumn signature on the country landscape as the fall leaves unveiled their many hues, while at the same time man's handsome architecture left its own signature on the history of time.

When I wasn't distracted by the scenery, I managed to plot a productive timetable to continue my question-and-answer process. I needed to stay away from lighthearted activities so I could stick with events that would permit long, drawn out, deep conversations.

When we arrived at Jim's condo, I smiled as I walked in and noticed a blanket and pillow placed neatly at the end of the sofa. Jim immediately took my suitcase upstairs to his room without a word.

As he returned from upstairs, I asked, "Can we go for a walk and kick a few leaves?"

"You certainly are in good spirits," he said as he looked at me suspiciously with that one-sided smile of his that indicated he had much more on his mind than walking.

"Why don't we just sit on the couch and rest awhile," he said, pulling me down to sit next to him.

"Rest? After a two-and-a-half-hour plane ride, a tranquil lunch, and a two-hour car ride in the country, now you want me to rest! If I sit still very much longer, I'll fall asleep."

"That wouldn't be so bad, would it?" he asked as he put his arm around me, pulling me close to him. "Just for a little while," he pleaded.

"OK." I conceded. Once again my please-everyone-else-first attitude was coming through. Just once, I wished I had the courage or confidence to insist on my own way. Well, I decided, if we were just going to sit here, I'm going to get to work on my mental question list.

"Let's talk," I said.

"I've got a better idea. You talk, and I'll listen," he said, as he gently leaned over and kissed my neck. I purposefully ignored his gesture and twisted myself around so I could look directly into his face. I may have compromised taking a walk, but I would not compromise my plan!

"You know, Jim, as often as we've talked on the phone, I still don't know much about you."

"What do you want to know?" he asked, his head now resting on my shoulder.

"I want to know all about you. Where you came from, where you're going, what your dreams are."

"That's pretty deep stuff for a Saturday afternoon."

"OK. Then let's start with some easier questions. Are you and your sister close? Where does your sister live? How is your relationship with her?"

"Slow down! You're making me dizzy. Where did this information crusade come from?"

"I want to know if we're compatible. I don't want to fall in love with you and then find out we are incompatible. Trust me, that's far too painful."

"Well," he crooned, "if we're going to get intimate, I need to get more comfortable."

I couldn't help feeling a little annoyed. Was he just toying with me, or was this his poor attempt at humor? I watched as he took off his sweater, then his shoes. He unbuttoned the sleeves of his lightly starched shirt and rolled them up. Then he unbuttoned a few buttons down the front of his shirt, revealing the dark hair on his manly chest.

I suddenly found myself reciting the last part of the Lord's prayer—"*Lead us not into temptation.*" If Jim thought he could distract me with his subtle seductive gestures, he was absolutely right. Yes, I had to admit I had a lustful side. O God, you sure knew what You were doing when You created man. I think Michelangelo and I shared the same appreciation for the male body.

Jim smiled as he laid on the sofa with his head in my lap. I took a deep breath and gulped down my thoughts in an effort to concentrate on my mission. Even though we were both sitting on the same sofa, we obviously had different objectives. Our communication wavelengths were miles apart, but at least Jim showed signs of compliance, even if he wasn't sincere.

He began his life history by working through a pretty normal childhood and led into some unfortunate relationships that had developed within his family. I saw the sadness set in as he began exposing his true heart to me. I wanted to reach out and console him as he expressed his pain. Somehow that didn't seem appropriate. He barely scratched the surface of his story when his uneasiness overwhelmed him. He jumped up and decided we would go for that walk instead.

I hadn't planned on the feeling of intimacy created by this exposure. Maybe I should take his advice and slow down with my questions. But still the questions flooded my mind. Why did he stop short of revealing himself? Was he protecting me or himself? Maybe he didn't trust me yet. Maybe he didn't want to share himself with me. Maybe he defined my purpose in his life much differently than I did. Was I ready to ask myself the question, *Why am I in his life?* In a word, no!

I left Philly the next day with more questions than I'd come with. I wasn't sure if I would be back to see Jim ever again. Maybe our relationship just wasn't meant to be.

Now that my spiritual life seemed back on track, I'd come to grasp a simple but monumental fact. My confidence no longer hinged on what others thought or felt about me, but on how I thought and felt about myself. Understanding this one fact freed me from a self-induced anxiety in which I had been unable to escape.

An unexplainable peace renewed my life. My new church not only gave me a place to belong, but genuine friends waited to hear from me. For the first time in a long time, I felt at peace with myself and hopeful for the future.

Jim's telephones calls persisted. The distance between us became more than a geographical one. He sensed my interest fading. Winning my attention became a bigger challenge, so he became more aggressive in his pursuit. His persistence sparked my curiosity, motivating me to ask, "Jim, realistically, where do you see our relationship heading?"

He surprised me by responding, "I was hoping it would lead to a walk down the aisle."

Wow! This guy was serious. Had I misjudged the situation that badly? Obviously he took our relationship more seriously than I thought. With this revelation I felt I owed our relationship a more serious consideration.

I agreed to fly to Philly to reevaluate our relationship. Hopefully this third trip would procure answers to many questions. First and foremost I needed to know the purpose of this relationship? If Jim was to be part of my life, I wanted to know why? What did we have to offer each other? Would we compliment each other? And why Philadelphia? God knows how much I detest cold weather.

For the full day and a half I would be in Philly, I committed myself to get inside this man's head to see what he was all about. Was there any bond at all, or was he just someone to fill in a temporary void?

Now that I was concentrating on my own internal restoration, the understanding of my relationships became much more important. I wanted to live up to the person I was becoming. I was just getting to know the new me.

Unfortunately, Jim's plans for the weekend were different from mine. Only through hindsight did I realize that he was determined to create a bond between us, something to tie us together.

When I arrived early that Saturday morning, Jim embraced me tighter than ever before. Emotionally he appeared to have taken a step closer to me, while I had taken a step away from him.

Jim took me to the same French Cafe as he had on my previous trip to Philly. He knew how much I enjoyed it. Obviously the courtship was still very much alive. He was trying to push all the right buttons to keep our relationship humming.

"Jim are you trying to spoil me?" I asked.

"If I thought that would be enough to keep you here, I would do my best."

"What about common interests? Isn't that important?" I asked.

"We have common interests. We both like each other, good food, and having fun together."

"I share those same interests with my dog, but I wouldn't marry him."

"Touche!" he laughed. "I suppose I deserved that."

We left the restaurant and headed to Jim's house. Jim opened up conversationally as never before. He outlined in detail his entire family history. Then he went on to tell me about three of his past female relationships, explaining why they didn't work out. He informed me he was a Catholic and that he went to church most Sundays. He loved to golf and watch sports. He had never been married or even engaged, and he had no children that he was aware of.

I said, "Wow! Once you decide to open up, you do a thorough job of it. But what button do I push to slow down the output of information?"

"You said you wanted to know all about me."

Laughing I said, "Yes, I do, but not in thirty minutes."

When we arrived at the house, we sat on the sofa to continue the disclosure process. Jim divulged information while I asked questions intermittently. We then began to compare our individual lifestyles. I pointed out our differences; Jim concentrated on our similarities.

"I'm sorry, Jim, but I am afraid to get any more involved with you because I just don't see us enjoying a successful future together. To be honest I'm really not even quite sure I've completely healed from my last relationship. But lately my life seems to have taken a refreshing new direction. The good news is that my spiritual life has grown tremendously, and it's affecting my everyday life. I'm finding real contentment in what I'm learning about relationships through my new-found relationship with God. I believe my spiritual development is the key to my emotional fulfillment."

I sensed my words were falling on deaf ears. We sat there a few minutes in silence. Jim knew he couldn't compete with *God*, but he wasn't giving up without a good fight. He responded with his best asset, his charm.

"You are so special," Jim said in a tone that told me he meant it. "I still remember the first day I saw you at the convention. I spotted you from across the room. You possessed a class that made you stand out in the crowd. Determined to meet you, I needed to make sure you weren't with someone before I approached you. Once I was able to talk to you, I saw through your meticulous appearance as you stood there elegantly in your tailored suit. I sensed your vulnerability."

"You made me uncomfortable. You were like a hawk after prey."

"Was I that obvious?" he asked as he began to kiss my cheeks, my nose, my chin, then he moved down to my neck.

"Yes, much like you are right now. You are not making this any easier for me," I said, trying to make light of the situation.

"Why should I make this easy for you. I want you to be part of my life," he said, as he kissed me passionately. I could feel the heat coming from his body as he pressed against me. Then he slowly began to rub his hands up and down my thighs. He looked me straight in the eyes just inches from my face and breathed, "You would look great on my arm wherever I go. You possess such grace and charm, you'd be a great asset to me as well as to my career."

The seduction was well underway. Suddenly I found myself on the floor. Jim proceeded with his attempt to bond us together, whatever it took. It all happened so fast. I tried to position my arms in a way that would allow for some leverage, knowing that my strength was unequal to his. I tried to push him off me. I did not want to have sex. I wanted to be treated with respect. I'd given too much of myself away in the past, and it was robbing me of my wholeness. For the first time I realized that intercourse was meant to be special and holy, not cheaply or randomly given.

God, please help me! I cried out inside myself.

I lay there on his living room floor, helplessly staring at the ceiling until Jim had finished satisfying himself.

Once again I had put someone else's desires before my own. Where was my fighting spirit? What was it about this situation that stripped me of my ability to stand up for what I knew was right? Was I so insecure that I would trade sex for flattery? I lay there feeling used and ashamed. I blamed myself. Why had I placed myself in this vulnerable position, so far from home, spending the weekend in a man's house, a man I barely knew? And why did I feel like I deserved respect?

The ordeal finally ended when Jim rolled over, jumped up, and said, "Let's go to a movie."

I stared at this strange man, searching for regret, remorse, maybe even an apology for his inability to control himself, but there was nothing. I could tell by his expression that he didn't have a clue.

But the bigger mystery lay in these questions: Why didn't I scream at him, No! And afterwards, why didn't I speak up and tell him how he made me feel? My confusion and brokenness had put me in an even more precarious position because now I couldn't even think clearly. He had all the advantages. I was on his turf, twenty miles outside a strange city, two thousand miles from home.

Few words were spoken between us the rest of the evening. I spoke only when spoken to. I acted like a mouse hovering in the corner, overshadowed by a huge cat that had blocked my only exit. I decided to stay in my corner until morning when I could make a run for it. Maybe if I was real quiet, he would just go away and leave me alone.

I remember that we went to a movie, but I couldn't tell you the name of it or anything about it. All emotion and feelings had drained from me. After the movie, I told Jim I didn't feel well. I went to bed.

The next morning I asked Jim to take me straight to the airport so I could catch an earlier flight.

"I'm not feeling well. I really need to get home."

"Is there anything I can do for you?"

Of course I wanted to say, "No, you've done quite enough!" But I restrained myself.

When we arrived at the airport, I saw a friend of mine at the ticket counter who worked with me in Dallas. I was anxious to talk with *anyone*, so I wouldn't have to talk to Jim before my flight left. We talked right up until flight time and I had to hurry to my gate. Jim was right there. We arrived in the departure area just as my flight was boarding.

"Well, Jim, you know I hate good-byes, so I'll be on my way."

He embraced me tightly, whispering, "I'll miss you."

I stood rigidly, without putting down my bags, coldly allowing but not reciprocating his embrace.

"I hope you feel better soon. Call me when you get home," he said as I boarded my flight.

Rain pounded like tears from heaven on the roof of the plane the whole flight home. I thought if I dared begin to cry, my tears might never stop. All my senses tingled as the vision of the night before played over and over in my mind. The smell of his breath, the weight of his body on mine, the pain of his disrespect. All those sensations crystallized indelibly upon my memory. How could I put the memory of Jim and that night behind me?

At that moment I determined that I would never see Jim Rebel again. As the plane landed, I arrived in Dallas feeling defiled, ashamed, and alone. I didn't want to talk to anyone. I wanted to lose myself in the crowd forever. I rushed from the airport to the safety of my apartment. Then I cried. I cried for a very long time. I blamed myself for my stupidity. I knew I got what I deserved. My relationship with Jim was a result of my irresponsible actions. Why did I ever go to Philadelphia? Why did I agree to stay in his home? *I set myself up!*

Although I accepted accountability for my own actions, I was still angry with Jim for his utter insensitivity to my feelings. But without my cooperation, his seduction wouldn't have taken place. Therefore, he couldn't hold the total blame.

I stood staring out my bedroom window, drowning in guilt. I listened to the heavy rain beating on the roof. My shame rose from deep within me. The relentless rains and powerful winds called to mind nature's own raging struggle. The autumn leaves hung on the trees for dear life as the wind blew them mercilessly. I felt like a leaf hanging on for dear life while the winds of adversity attempted to rip me from any source of stability.

Any other day I would have enjoyed the rain. To me, it symbolized the earth's natural cleansing process. But that day my perspective was much different. The rain seemed cruel and unrelenting as it stripped the vibrant colored leaves in their peak of brilliance. The vulnerable leaves were overpowered, and plucked from their only source of sustaining life, they fell hopelessly to the ground.

I identified with the fallen leaves lying on the cold, hard ground. I, like the leaf, was only one among many who suffered the pain of an inconsideration. Lying on my bed like a fallen leaf, I had a singular prospective. The only view I had from way down below was *up*.

CHAPTER 3

He Took My Hand
and Said, "Come"

fter two weeks of not answering the door or my phone, my neighbor Tom knocked on my door. He was a nice looking fellow from the singles group at church. We had visited on several occasions. We talked about everything and nothing. But most of our conversations ended up including some type of related spiritual insight. I could tell Tom was interested in helping me in my spiritual walk, but he never pushed the issue. His everyday life seemed naturally one with his spiritual life. His perspective on life in general intrigued me. He exuded confidence and peacefulness that enhanced his already neat appearance.

When I opened my door Tom stood there with a big, warm smile, "Hey, stranger. What's been going on?"

"Hi, Tom. Come in."

"I haven't seen you at church or even around here for a while. I asked Carmen if she'd heard from you. She said she hadn't seen you either."

"I was out of town a couple of weekends ago, and I've been trying to recover ever since."

"Wow! That must have been some weekend, "Tom declared.

"You have no idea!"

"Do you want to talk about it?"

"I think I would like to, but it's pretty embarrassing."

"If you need an ear, I'm listening. I doubt you could tell me anything I haven't already experienced or heard about."

"Well, I could use a friend right now," I said weakly. "I think I've lost all objectivity."

Tom sat down and leaned toward me very attentively. "Tell me what happened."

I sat there in silence for a few minutes, struggling for words. Just thinking about it brought back all the pain. This was going to be harder than I thought. What would he think of me? Well, he probably wouldn't think anything that wasn't the truth, so why not just get it over with. There was no turning back now.

"I'm afraid I acted pretty irresponsibly. But God doesn't need to punish me, because Satan is right here to make sure I pay and keep on paying for it."

"Deborah," he said very softly, "God knew every mistake you and I would ever make in our whole lives, and He still sent His Son to die for us to redeem those mistakes. Jesus already paid for your mistakes."

"Tom, that sounds good, but you'd better hear what happened before you say anymore. I'm sure even God has limits to what He tolerates."

"Nothing you can tell me will make any difference. But if it will help you to talk about it, I'll be glad to listen."

So I unleashed the whole disgusting story. I didn't

dare look at Tom as I spoke for fear I would see disappointment in his eyes. Then we sat there in silence for what seemed like a hundred years. Finally, Tom broke the silence.

"Deb, the devil doesn't always carry a pitchfork and have a tail. He is the prince of deception. He knows where we are weak, and he focuses on those vulnerable areas. He is wise, cunning, and he attacks when he feels threatened. What have you done to make him mad lately?"

We both laughed. I felt such relief at Tom's acceptance and understanding.

"I hate to be the one to tell you this, but I think it's your church attendance that's got Satan upset," Tom offered.

"Well, Satan sure fixed that didn't he. I haven't been back since I was snared in his trap. Now I'm too ashamed to go back. I feel like such a hypocrite!"

"Deborah, don't let Satan win. What Jim did was wrong in the eyes of God. Jim is responsible for his actions, and you are responsible for yours. But don't let Jim stand between you and your relationship with God. If Jim stands between you and God, he's one step closer to God than you."

"Tom you may be right about Jim, but since I'm already in the confessional, so to speak, I can't let you go away thinking that I'm totally virtuous. I'm afraid I've fallen from grace more times than I would ever be willing to admit, even to myself."

Tom's answer surprised me.

"I know just how you feel. When I first came to the Lord, my sin closet was so full I was afraid to open the door. I'd been storing them for some time. The enemy convinced me, that if I just didn't acknowledge my sins, they would sit silently in the closet and leave me alone.

"However the truth was that the mere weight of my sins kept me from attaining God's best for my life. Sin stole my ability to be totally honest, and the ability to enjoy the blessings of God."

"What did you do?"

"Thank God, someone told me that all unconfessed sin separates us from God and keeps us from being redeemed, forgiven, and free! But fear kept me from the Father's arms."

"I know all about fear."

"But Deb, *all* fear comes from the devil himself. I just knew that once I disclosed all my sins, God would throw up His hands and send me straight to hell. But I also knew if my life continued in the same direction, I would be going to hell anyway—and a lot sooner than I planned."

"You? You were a bad guy? And just what did you do that was so bad? Skip church?"

"Well, we don't have time to get into my past. But trust me when I say it was the confession of my sins that cured my life threatening illness. The sickness of sin can eat away at a person until there is nothing left but death.

God said, *Let the wicked forsake his way and the evil man his thoughts. Let him turn to the Lord, and he will have mercy on him, and to our God, for he will freely pardon* (Isaiah 55:7).

"Man, was I glad the day I read that!" Tom said.

"So just like that, you were free, forgiven, and living happily ever after?"

"Oh, no! I didn't buy all this Jesus stuff so easily. It was a slow process. There was so much for me to learn. Such as, being a Christian didn't mean I would never sin again. Be assured, I did. And when I did sin, the gentle Spirit of God was there to make me aware of my sin. It seemed as if I were pedaling backward for a long time. The closer I got to God the more sin I saw in my life. I thought I must be doing something very wrong, because before I knew God I thought I was a pretty nice person. All of a sudden everywhere I turned I realized another sin. A loving God was exposing me as a helpless sinner."

"That sounds painful."

"It's not easy, and if anyone tells you it is, they are not doing it right. By exposing us to ourselves a little at a time, God gently humbles us enough to convince us to exchange our lives for His. But we have to get to a point of total surrender before God can begin to do great things through us."

"Things like saving your neighbor from the depths of despair?"

"Maybe," Tom smiled.

When he left that night, I knew I wanted the same kind of peace and wisdom I saw in Tom. He possessed a wisdom that kept him out of trouble and a peace that convinced me I was missing something very significant in my life. I wanted that same kind of wisdom and peace. Now to find it.

JESUS MET ME AT THE WELL

Sunday morning one week later, I walked into church with a renewed purpose. I didn't know exactly *how* to start my new crusade, but I knew *where* to start.

Carmen faithfully met me at the door, and we went into the sanctuary. She knew I liked to sit toward the back, so she graciously slid into a back row. I gently grabbed her arm and whispered, "Let's go up to the front today."

She smiled and gestured for me to lead the way. I

chose the second row of the center section.

The message that day came from the fourth chapter of the Book of John, the story of the Samaritan woman who came to the well where Jesus was sitting. The pastor's message went like this:

> As Jesus rested by the well, He asked a Samaritan woman for a drink of water. This woman was astonished when Jesus asked her for a drink. In those days, a Jewish Rabbi would never speak to a woman in public, not even his wife or daughter. Women were considered inferior to men.
>
> It was also common knowledge that Jews despised Samaritans. Under Jewish law, even this woman's water vessel was considered unclean for Jewish drinking. And yet Jesus spoke to this woman at the well without appearing theologically or racially superior but as an equal. Jesus' kindness complimented the woman and induced her receptiveness to His words. Jesus peered deep into her heart. He knew her thirst for spiritual knowledge exceeded that of her physical body. So Jesus offered her living water—a perpetual spring with eternal life. He was inviting her into His Kingdom where all her needs would be met.
>
> So that the Samaritan woman might believe in Him, Jesus divulges her past to her. He speaks to her living arrangements, revealing her five husbands and discloses the fact that she is now living with a man who is not her husband. The woman was overwhelmed. She thought at the very least, He was a prophet.

The woman said she was waiting for the Messiah to come and that He would answer all their spiritual questions. That's when Jesus said, *"I am the Messiah!"* The woman left her water jar and ran to be a witness for the Lord.

Why did Jesus choose a woman with a reputation to be His messenger? Surely if Jesus wanted to spread the word that He was on earth He could have used a more reputable emissary. Isn't that just like Him to do things that seem backwards and illogical to us?

Jesus never followed the way things ought to be. He always charted His own course, and His courses were always right on the mark. He saw this woman as so much more than she saw herself. Satan had taken years to pervert her life and set her on a path of destruction, yet during a five-minute conversation, Jesus broke her bondage with a gift—the ultimate gift of love through compassion and forgiveness. But He also gave her the truth—the very truth that would set her free to be all she could be. The compassion opened her heart and the truth was able to enter and set her free.

Can you imagine how this woman's life changed after she came face to face with the Messiah, the Savior of the world?

I'm sure she asked herself many times, "Why me? What did Jesus see in me besides darkness and sin? I'm nobody special."

Well, I'm here to tell you, you are special. Every one of you is special and God can use you right where you are to complete His plan.

He is waiting to reclaim what is rightfully His. God desires for you to see yourself through His eyes so that you can be used to enhance His kingdom. You are already equipped to do all that God has called you to do. You just need to choose your Boss today and begin to live out what God has planned for you. Go in peace to love and serve the Lord!

I felt as if the pastor stared right at me during the entire sermon. Convinced I was the only person he was talking to, I looked around to see if everyone else was looking at me. But everyone appeared to be listening just as intently. Maybe they were just being polite.

Although the name of the woman is never mentioned, I called her Deborah. Surely God could see my seeking heart and meet me at my point of need. I wanted to personally hear His voice and feel His compassion just like the Samaritan woman.

I leaned over to Carmen sitting next to me and said, "I want to sit and talk to Jesus just like her."

Carmen said with a smile, "You can!"

"How?" I asked.

"All you have to do is learn to recognize Him."

I sat speechless with my eyes wide open. Carmen's words slowly replaying over and over in my mind, I looked up at the cross hanging high in the front of the sanctuary as if I were seeing it with new eyes. I noticed that it was empty! After sitting there staring for sometime, I began to smile. This was it! This was just what I had been searching for—a living God! Not one that was still on the cross. But One with whom I could relate because He is alive!

I didn't know how to recommit my life to God.

Certainly if my heart was willing, the Lord would show me the way. As a non-conformer, I didn't want to ask anyone the proper way to renew my faith. I wanted all my prompting to come from the Spirit of God. I had seen a lot of dramatic actions from seemingly civilized people on television, everything from falling down, to wailing, and various other strange responses. I just wanted to quietly make my peace with God and begin to live.

I heard people often came to the altar to make their commitment or recommitment. This public confession signified their accountability before God and the church body. That made perfect sense. I suppose if I didn't have the guts to walk up to the altar and confess my faith in front of a church full of Christians, how would I ever make a stand of faith out in the cold, cruel world of reality?

The church was full that Sunday evening in early October. I decided this was as good a time as any, and I went to the altar and knelt. And in silent prayer from my heart, I said:

"Father God, I don't know if I'm doing this right, but I need You to do something with my life. I've made a mess of it. I'm suppose to have a heart, but I have hardened it so deeply You may have to do a transplant. I promise if You give me a new heart, I will take much better care of it.

Tonight I want to rededicate my life to You. I've always professed Christianity in my head, but now I want to be a Christian in my heart. I not only want a new heart but also a new life. A life that no longer just includes You, but a life that imitates Your character.

The burden of my sins are too heavy. Please forgive me and relieve my guilt."

As I knelt there in the presence of a church full of people, it seemed as though only God and I were in this peaceful place. Then something indescribable happened. I experienced an incredible soothing, warmth literally flood my entire being. It was as though God's Spirit came to rest inside me. I knew without a doubt my life would never be the same!

By the time I returned to my seat more than half of the congregation had already left the church. But there sat my faithful friend, Carmen. I don't know whose smile was wider, hers or mine. She motioned for me to sit down next to her.

"What happened?"

With tears of joy still bathing my face, I said, "I asked God to help me. I asked Him to forgive me and to give me a new heart. His heart. As I was praying, the pastor laid his hands on me. That's when it happened."

"What happened?"

"A warm sensation filled my body. It was as if all my unworthiness was lifted and I felt holy." Hearing those words come out of me, I could hardly believe it. And I said, " Kind of crazy, huh?"

"No, not at all," Carmen beamed. "You've experienced a spiritual rebirth."

And for the first time in my life, I enjoyed sharing my spiritual experience. I now knew this **was** something to be shared.

"Does this mean that I'm one of those Jesus freaks now?" I asked.

"Not necessarily, Carmen answered. "But it is important to know that you are just a baby Christian and growing up spiritually is a process. Don't expect to lose all of your sinful habits by tomorrow. Being reborn spiritually means you no longer have a past in the eyes of God. Babies don't have a past. God looks at you as an innocent babe. Let me show you what 2 Corinthians 5:17 says: *Therefore, if anyone is in Christ he is a new creation; the old has gone, the new has come!"*

I knew I needed Carmen now more than ever to answer all of my questions and help me with spiritual direction.

"What am I suppose to do now?" I asked.

"Keep an open heart and a teachable spirit. Just like a baby, you'll need to eat to grow. You will want to feed on the Word of God to grow spiritually. Take small steps, and don't expect too much too soon. As a baby Christian, you will take some falls as you try to stand and eventually walk. But be patient. It took you a long time to be comfortable in your current lifestyle. Give God time to work with you as He transforms your character."

"That sounds easy enough."

"Sometimes it's the easiest thing in the world; but when you fall or fail, it will hurt. Don't give up, and know where to turn for renewed strength."

"How can you be so sure I will fall?"

"We all fall short of God's expectations from time to time, even our pastors. King David, who was a man after God's heart, committed serious sins against God. And Peter the Apostle, one of Jesus' most faithful followers denied Him three times.

"I'm not to trying to discourage you by any means, Debi. Quite the opposite. I just don't want you to expect too much too soon and get discouraged. Godly character is not easily achieved. If it were easy, everybody would have it. But I'm happy to tell you it's well worth every bump and bruise along the way."

"I'm not sure whether to be happy or depressed."

"Oh! Rejoice for sure, but be aware the road isn't all uphill."

I don't know how long we talked. I do know that the sanctuary was empty. We were both surprised at the lateness of the hour. So Carmen took hold of my hand and said, "Debi, will you call me if you need someone to talk to?"

"You can count on that."

We hugged each other and left church that night filled with hope and gratitude.

I was thirsty, and like the woman of Samaria, I came to the well. Jesus met me there and filled my spirit with so much more than water. My life would never be the same again.

⚜⚜⚜⚜⚜⚜⚜⚜⚜

You too may feel like the woman at the well. You may have that aching void in you and wish to be filled with joy and purpose. It can be just as easy for you as it was for me. Just have a willing heart and a committed spirit.

God made you just the way you are. Not only did God create you, but He scheduled every day of your life before you were born (Psalm 139:16, TLB). He has also given you the power to choose whom and what you will follow. Come, Jesus waits for you!

If you have never asked Jesus Christ to come into your heart, and you want to; or if you are a Christian and want to renew your walk with the Lord, just pray the following prayer with feeling and belief from your heart:

"Lord Jesus, I know I am a sinner and need Your forgiveness. I believe You died for my sins. I confess my sins and turn from them. I now invite You into my heart and life. I trust You as my Savior and Lord of my life. Thank You for forgiving my sins and giving me eternal life. Amen."

That's it. If you meant every word you just prayed, you are now a BORN AGAIN Christian. You have been adopted into God's family. You can now look forward to receiving your full inheritance. It is also important to find another child of God to share your experience with. As you grow spiritually, you will have many questions, and choosing this narrow path is not always easy. But it is definitely worth the effort.

> Verily, verily, I say unto thee. Except a man be born again, he cannot see the kingdom of God.
>
> —JOHN 3:3, KJV

CHAPTER 4

"O God—It's Blue!"

For weeks Jim left messages on my home answering machine. The sound of his voice reminded me of a lifestyle I was content to leave behind. It wasn't until he reached me at work that I knew I must face the inevitable. How else could I get him out of my life forever?

Although Jim's call caught me off guard, it didn't surprise me. Maybe work was the perfect place for me to deal with him. I was safe here. I could put on my best professional voice and try to reason out an unreasonable situation. After all, I was trained for public relations. I had to use tact and courtesy, state my position, and stand firm. I couldn't let my emotions muddle things up. Now, if only my voice would cooperate, remain controlled, and not reveal my racing pulse.

I saw only one way to stop Jim from calling, and that was to teach him the meaning of the words, "The End. It's over." On that basis I accepted his call.

I picked up the phone reluctantly. The familiar voice penetrated my veneer. Instantly I was out of control as the events of our last evening together came flooding back into my mind.

"Hello, this is Deborah, how can I help you?" I said with professionalism, acting as though I didn't know who was on the other end of the receiver.

"Hi, I've been worried about you."

"Oh! Hello Jim. I've been very busy, in and out of town."

"Deborah, is something going on I should know about?"

I couldn't help my sarcastic thought, *Oh, he finally noticed! What a sensitive man!*

Getting right to the point, I said, "Jim, this just isn't going to work."

"We haven't given it enough time yet, Deborah."

"I don't think it's *time* we need, but an objective evaluation. You know, Jim, happily-ever-afters don't just happen because two people get along well. There is so much more to consider."

"Like what?"

"Well, let's just start with our spiritual differences. As I told you when I was in Philly last time, my spiritual life has taken top priority. This isn't a hobby I pursue only on Sunday. It's a way of life. The same way of life I want to share with the man I marry and spend the rest of my life with."

"Deb, you know I wouldn't keep you from pursuing your religion. I think religion is good. It keeps us out of trouble."

"Jim, I need more than tolerance of my first amend-ment rights. I need someone to honor as well as to participate in my daily Christian lifestyle. Let's face it. We don't have enough going for us to compensate for the sacrifices we would face together."

"What sacrifices?"

His response told me he hadn't given this situation much thought. Jim appeared totally oblivious to the sacrifices that would be involved to join our lives together. Of course that meant he hadn't even considered making any of the necessary sacrifices himself. Had he assumed I would make them all?

"Are *you* willing to move to Dallas? Are *you* willing to give up *your* career, *your* family, and *your* friends for me?"

"Well, this surprises me. You know I couldn't do that."

"So you assumed I would give up *my* career, *my* family, and *my* friends to move to Philadelphia to be with you? I would give up twelve years of service with American Airlines, as well as *my* church, *my* friends, and *my* goal of moving up in this company? Is that what you're saying, Jim?"

"Well, not exactly. I guess I haven't thought it all through."

After a few minutes of silence, Jim continued, "Can't you just transfer with American to Philadelphia?"

"Why?" I paused, hoping he might take time to consider what he was asking me to do. His insensitivity began to anger me. He didn't answer, so I plunged on.

"In the first place," I replied, "I detest cold weather. Secondly, you are the only person I know in Philadelphia. And finally, to be honest with you, there is just not enough between us to even motivate that consideration."

I heard him sigh. After a few moments of uncomfortable silence, he said, "Is that it?"

"Yes."

"Well, Debi, if you change your mind, would you please call me?"

"I promise you'll be the first to know," I said in my most unsympathetic tone.

But even at that, he decided to take another stab, "You're not doing this just so you can date Bill Noble again are you?"

"As I said before, Bill and I have a platonic friendship."

"OK," he said in a semi-defeated way. "Can I call you once in a while to see how you're doing?"

"Sure. I wish you well in your career but I really have to get back to work."

"Good-bye, Deborah, but will you please keep in touch?"

I made no promise. I wanted to forget that relationship and mark it up to experience, an experience not worth repeating. Live and learn they say.

Just then a friend and coworker, Marla, tapped me on the shoulder.

"Man trouble?" she asked.

"Not anymore. Cross another one off the list."

"I just wish I had your list."

"No you don't. Men are a lot more trouble than they're worth. Take it from someone who knows. Single life sounds soothing."

"You have to give yourself time to get over the old wounds before you try to move forward. It's obvious to me you're still trying to find a replacement for the last big relational void in your life."

"You have no idea."

"I think I do. I'm single, not stoic." We both laughed.

"I'm sorry Marla, I didn't mean to imply that you couldn't relate. Thinking about my past relationships throws me into a futile pity party."

"Sorry! Those kinds of parties I don't attend. They are a total waste of time and precious energy. Besides, they insult my Father, God."

"Your what?" I asked surprised by the foreign language I heard coming from someone I thought I knew.

"My heavenly Father—you know the guy in charge upstairs, the big Pilot in the sky."

This was the first time I'd heard Marla express her belief in God. We had spent many lunch hours and late evenings talking about everything, at least everything but God. We also took several trips together, but never had we shared our thoughts about spiritual matters.

"Marla, are you a Christian?"

"I'm sorry you had to ask."

"Why?"

"I'm suppose to be a witness for Jesus by the way I live. You shouldn't have had to ask me. Spiritual boldness is not an attribute I practice enough. I suppose my queen size physique, along with my nickname 'Brain,' already isolate me enough. I'm afraid if I adopt one more tag that sets me apart, I won't have anyone to talk to in this office."

"You mean you actually have people who to talk to you here at work?"

"Sure they all talk to me when they want to know something or they don't understand the latest computer enhancement, but after hours you'd think I had the plague. The only reason they don't talk to you is because they know you're the new rookie who appears to be the front-runner for the next sales rep job. That's a job they would all kill for."

"Oh? The rumors are flying, huh? They have the

same opportunity as I to interview for the position, you know."

"Don't bet on it. Many of them have tried it, but 'zip!' It's easier for them to blame you than it is for them to take responsibility for their own inabilities."

"I don't want to hear this."

"I think you should. It will make your short stay here more tolerable if you understand and thus forgive."

"What are you talking about, religion or my job?"

"Both. I'm going out of character here and attempt spiritual boldness."

"Lucky me."

"Humor me here. Besides, it's good practice for me."

"OK, shoot."

"Debi, do you believe in God?"

"Yes! Much more lately than ever before ."

"Do you believe in Jesus Christ as your personal Lord and Savior?"

"Sure. I'm a Christian. I was raised Catholic!"

"Deborah, being Catholic doesn't make you a Christian. It's not about belonging to a denomination, it's about belonging to God and assuming a godly character. It's about a relationship just like you and your best friend."

"I don't have a best friend. You see, to have a best friend I'd have to trust someone totally. I've only had two best friends in my life, both, way back in high school."

"Tell me about them."

"A best friend is like an extension of yourself. You share everything and become totally vulnerable to them. The payoff for such a risky relationship comes when you know someone else shares the same pain or joy you do. It intensifies your joy and divides your pain."

"Debi, that's exactly the kind of relationship Jesus wants to have with us. That's why He chose to come to earth as a baby and grow up the same way we did, so He could experience the same everyday trials we do. He wants to be part of our everyday lives. Even here in this office, He wants to make your life easier."

"That's pretty heavy. I'll have to chew on that for a while."

"I understand. Growing spiritually takes time, and it goes against our rebellious nature but you haven't struck me as one who follows the crowds or does anything the easy way."

"You got that right."

Marla started to walk away when my curiosity got the best of me. "Marla," I called.

"Yeah?" She stopped and turned toward me. I walked up to her and softly asked, "What made you bold today and why with me?"

"I overheard the end of your private phone conversation as I passed your desk. I thought you could use a friend. The rest just happened."

"Just happened, huh?"

"I really had no ulterior motive. I wanted to console you but when we, as Christians, are faithful to God, He allows us to be His arms and sometimes His mouth."

"Did you know I was attending a new church?"

"Cassie mentioned it to me. I guess that's why I felt the freedom to share what was on my heart."

"It seems like lately God is really trying to get my attention."

"That's great, Debi!"

"Not always. It seems I'm up against some pretty

evil stuff as well."

"That's good too!"

"Oh, no it's not. It's awful."

"You're being fought over."

"You know, Marla, Tom, my neighbor who goes to the same church I do, has told me, basically, the same thing."

"If God is trying to get your attention then you must be seeking the truth."

"He said that, too. Marla, you have exposed a whole new side of you. I like it. I would love to talk to you more about this later."

"What are you doing tonight?"

"Well, I haven't been feeling very good lately. I think I've got a bug that I just can't seem to shake. But I'll call you in a few days."

"Great! I'll wait to hear from you."

FLU SYMPTOMS?

Days, then weeks, went by. I still was unable to shake this "flu." My body was really acting strange. And why hadn't my period started? My periods were very regular unless I was under a lot of stress or flying a lot. Maybe this flu was messing up my system.

I waited another two weeks and nursed my symptoms. When my period still didn't start, I panicked. I counted the days and studied my calendar, attempting to pinpoint the dates I was in Philly.

O sweet Jesus! surely I couldn't be pregnant? I tried to deny any possibility that conception might have taken place. I suppose I even briefly considered ignoring the obvious evidence. I thought to myself, *I won't think about this now. I'll think about it tomorrow.* Surely this will all go away. But I needed some answers if I planned to ever sleep again.

I came to the conclusion that there was enough evidence to make that dreaded trip to the drugstore for a pregnancy test. Needless to say, I did not shop for the best price. Embarrassed and scared, I just picked up the first test I found and got out of there before I ran into someone I knew.

When I got home, I discovered to my horror that I'd bought a test that required waiting until morning to get an accurate reading! What a bummer! But I sure wasn't about to rush back to the drugstore to exchange it for one that produced quicker results.

Waiting through the night made the question of pregnancy more agonizing. My worry increased, and fear grew with each passing minute. After hours of convincing myself I was worrying about nothing, I finally closed my eyes and slept.

Before my eyes were fully opened the next morning, I jumped out of bed, and painstakingly followed the instructions on the box. Then I waited the longest ten minutes of my life. Then I looked. "O God! It's blue!" There it was! As blue as a summer sky. No ifs, ands, or buts about it, I was pregnant!

I stood in the cold confines of my bathroom staring into the mirror at a person who once seemed so familiar. Numb and removed from the rest of the world, I couldn't focus on anything.

After agonizing about the possibility of an unwanted, unplanned pregnancy for weeks, the reality left me overwhelmed. Not me! This only happens to other people. You know, the kind you hear about—young, careless, and unfortunate. Not to someone like me! Not a successful thirty-year-old professional woman who had everything going for her.

I stood in front of the mirror staring at this

stranger's reflection.

"Who are you?" I asked. "What have you become?" I thought, *I used to clearly see the plans for her future. I knew her dreams and aspirations.* Suddenly everything appeared fuzzy and her dreams shattered, replaced by nothing but heartache and disappointment.

I saw fear in her eyes. I reached out to comfort this stranger's troubled face, but I only felt the cold, hard glass before me. The reality of an unwanted pregnancy was met with bitter tears. Nothing could ever be the same again.

"O God, how could You do this to me? Why now? Why would You wait until I rededicated my life to You to create this life inside me? Why didn't You zap me with a child when I was out of your will and sexually promiscuous? That's when I deserved it. Not *now*! You know how hard I'm trying to live a good Christian life. What will people think once my sin is exposed?"

Thousands of thoughts and feelings raced through my mind. I felt scared, angry, confused, guilty, used, and somehow even strangely excited with the idea of a precious little person growing inside me. The miracle of life was taking place inside me. Oh, how I wished this life had been conceived out of love!

I reflected on the dreams of wanting children of my own, but my dreams were painted much differently. My dreams always included a loving husband. My own selfishness robbed the celebration of my child's birth and turned it into a crisis situation. I was angry! But upon whom was my anger directed? At me for my selfishness or at God for creating this life?

"God, You have more power than me. You know I have a weakness when someone offers to hold me and comfort me. I crave attention. It makes me feel significant, lovable, and temporarily fulfilled. But You are the essence of love and fulfillment. You create life. Why did You create this life? Is this my punishment? Is this child a victim of your wrath on my life? Would you do that to an innocent life?"

I think not. There must be another explanation. There had to be a reason beyond my understanding.

I struggled through my thoughts trying to justify my behavior. All the while I wished I could awaken from what I hoped was a bad dream.

The church talks about a spiritual transformation that takes place when a person rededicates their life to God, but I knew this physical transformation my body was about to encounter was not part of God's eternal plan.

How could I bring myself to go to work today? How long would it be before everyone would start looking at me funny? I had to somehow put this out of my mind for at least eight hours, or I wouldn't make it through my work day. My secret would be safe for a couple of months. This would be precious time needed to work through my plan of action. I would just keep myself too busy to think about it. I would plan a lot of out of town trips until I was ready to deal with reality.

I managed to get through the day somehow, and thank God, it was Friday! I couldn't seem to get beyond the question, "Why, God, why?

Of course, I had to admit it wasn't God who got me into this mess, but my own foolishness. Now standing face-to-face with the humility of my sinful nature, I realized I possessed no power of my own to live a godly life, nor could I measure up to God's standards with my own feeble strength. How, how could I present myself to a holy, righteous God and ask Him to forgive me when I knew I would go right out and sin again? My defensive nature would need time, as well as God's grace to face and deal with the consequences of my actions.

Here I sat, pregnant, unmarried and too ashamed to go back to church. I'd often heard girls question, "How could I be pregnant now? It was my *first* time!" Here I was saying, "How could I be pregnant now? It was my *last* time!"

Only two weeks ago I had committed myself to a new life and secured my relationship with God. I didn't want to disappoint Him ever again by getting sexually involved with a man outside the commitment of marriage. So why was I pregnant now? Why now, when I had trusted God for His gentle guidance in this area? Was this God's idea of gentle guidance?

I thought once I became a Christian, my life would be easier. I would just automatically stop sinning and doing things that weren't pleasing to the Lord. I believed that now God would fight my battles and administer justice to my enemies, and I would just go along for the ride.

My head was bombarded with questions and emotions as I thought, *How will I tell my mother? How am I going to tell my family? Where will I go? What will I do? What about my job? Who will understand?*

Panic exhausted me. The situation was too big to comprehend. Now more than any other time in my life, I was feeling alone and separated from those I loved and cared for. I was separated from my family. It wouldn't be long before I would be separated from my friends. And now, when I was finally finding peace in my spiritual life, I felt my sin would separate me from God.

As I prepared for bed that evening, I kept hearing the words, "Trust Me. Trust Me."

I knew how to obey God, but did I know how to trust Him? To establish trust I needed a personal relationship with Him. I knew I had some kind of relationship with Him but, was my relationship with God strong enough to pull me out of these circumstances? Somehow I had to reach up and bring Him down out of that lofty place in the sky where I'd kept Him most of my life. I needed to either bring Him down to my level or I would have to fly up to meet Him. But how could I face Him even if He met me halfway?

"O God have mercy! please don't allow my guilt to block my ability to receive Your love and forgiveness."

It was in the stillness of the night when I could hear a gentle voice inside me reassure me with bits of wisdom. I knew in my heart that God did not want me to feel used and ashamed. I thought about David in the Bible. He had committed murder *and* adultery, and yet God loved him, forgave him, and used him in a mighty way to do great things.

As I lay in bed at the end of the longest day of my life, I focused on the awesome love of God. I found peace— the peace I needed to close my eyes and finally rest.

WHAT NOW?

My weekend was full of reflection and prayer. I played Christian music on the stereo and pampered myself with food and relaxation. I turned on my answering machine and turned the volume down so I wouldn't hear any incoming message and be tempted to pick up the phone. I wanted to be alone just in case God had a message about how I was supposed to get out of this mess.

"I'm **pregnant**." Even the color of that word

changed somehow from bright and cheery to the color of sin—dark and dismal. What should have been a potential blessing was transformed into an ugly curse.

I thought of Eve in the Garden of Eden. I once considered Eve's deception as foolish. How could anyone be so easily tempted by the serpent's lies? My exact words resounded over and over in my ears, "How could anyone be so susceptible to a *snake?*" Oh, how my heart was full of compassion for her now!

I wasn't a teenager, nor was I dealing with the struggles that accompany young adulthood. Yet, facing this unwanted pregnancy made me feel like a child. I was supposed to be older and wiser, but I was just as devastated as if I were eighteen. The questions were all the same, and the answers were just as hard to find.

I remembered my mother once telling me that she served a stubborn God. She believed He had made her a promise that her faithfulness to Him would be rewarded by His faithfulness to her. He would never let go of her children. Oh, how I wanted to count on God's stubborn love. Somehow, my mother's once threatening promise turned into a gentle reassurance.

Where some sins could be forgotten, if not forgiven, my pregnancy could neither be denied or ignored.

I wondered why I was so insistent about giving God the credit for the creation of this life inside me, other than the fact it lifted the responsibility of my actions from me to God. Pretty convenient I'd say. How much credit could I give God for my pregnancy when I certainly hadn't given Him any real credit for the creation of my own life?

Of course, I was taught as a child in Bible classes to say God made me because God made everybody, but I hadn't considered my specific life being created by

God for a purpose.

Accepting the fact God had made Deborah for a specific purpose would take some convincing. I had grown up as one of many children in our family, so one of many people that God created was a comfortable concept for me. But I was a firm believer that it was indeed God who created me.

Once I accepted God as my Creator, why had I not followed my natural childlike inquisitiveness and continued with "Why?" How had this basic mystery escaped my persistent scrutinizing?

If God is responsible for my existence and He is a God of purpose, what was my purpose? God told Eve to be fruitful and multiply. If I was looking for a loophole to justify my present condition, this might be it. But my name wasn't Eve, and I was seeking much more than an excuse.

I reflected back on my childhood spiritual indoctrination and pressed my memory for the answers to those basic questions I recited in elementary Bible class. The teacher stood in front of the classroom and asked, "Who made you?"

We would all respond in unison, "God made me."

But what was the second question? Oh, yes! I remember now.

"Why did God make you?"

And we responded, "To love and serve the Lord."

Could the answer to fulfillment rest in that simple statement? Could I have missed the sole purpose of my existence? At the age of thirty, had I uncovered the key to real happiness that I literally searched the world for? If the answer was so simple, why had no one shared it with me? If someone did tell me, why had I not heard it with my heart or acted on it? Did it take the creation of this new life inside me to cause my mind to ponder this basic truth? Maybe my introspection had more to do with my spiritual rededication than my pregnancy. Was this the Spirit of God bringing me through a spiritual rebirth by starting my new life with the proper direction and purpose?

I opened my Bible to do a little research on my own. I started in the beginning of the Book of Genesis. Creation began when God gave everything He made, including man, a reason for being. It says He put His nature, image, and likeness in them.

Now there is something to live up to! We are created to be sons and daughters of God, to share His interests and visions. We were sitting pretty until the fall of man through disobedience or the big "S" word, "Sin." I suppose you could also use the word Satan, representing his victory over man.

Our (man's) disobedience broke God's heart and He threw us out of the Garden to show us there are consequences for sinfulness. How else could He claim to be a God of justice. But God loved us so much that He comes up with a plan to win us back into His good graces. He sends His only Son to die on the cross for our disobedience so that we can return to that Garden relationship.

The way I read the story of Jesus, He came to earth and reopened the gates of Eden. Now we have a choice. We are free to return as sons and daughters of God, or we can remain on the outside looking in with all our worldly treasures to make us materially happy. Could I be so content with material comfort that I would sacrifice my eternal happiness with God? The more questions I came up with the more confused I became.

I reflected on what Carmen had shared with me about failing God. However, this was a bigger failure than anything I had imagined. I was thinking along the lines of failing to go to church or failing to read the Bible. Failing to remain sexually pure hadn't entered my mind. Was there a sin that was too big for God to forgive? My questions would have to wait because the only way I could ask them would be to expose myself. I needed more time to adjust. The longer I sat alone with my thoughts and fears, the bigger they grew. I needed to know God had not left me to wallow in my fear and guilt. I was reminded of a definition of fear a friend once shared with me.

F = False
E = Evidence
A = Appearing
R = Real

The hopelessness I felt was false evidence—just a feeling, not the truth. The separation I felt wasn't from God, but Satan's false evidence planted on me like a parasite.

I needed some kind of reassurance that would carry more weight than my own reasoning. So I opened my Bible to the topic of separation, and I found:

> Who shall separate us from the love of Christ? Shall trouble or hardship or persecution or famine or nakedness or danger or sword?
>
> No, in all these things we are more than conquerors through him who loved us.
>
> For I am convinced that neither death nor life, neither angels nor demons, neither the present nor the future, nor any powers, neither height nor depth, nor anything else in all

creation, will be able to separate us from the
love of God that is in Christ Jesus our Lord.
—ROMANS 8:35, 37–39

It was amazing! Every time I went to the Bible for
direction, I became more and more convinced God
was with me. Not only through my current circumstance, but He wanted to encourage me in all aspects
of my life. He wanted me to be the best I could be and
for me to fulfill all of my dreams and expectations.
God's love appeared to have no conditions. No matter
what I had done in my life to disappoint Him, He still
loved me. All He required was for me to ask forgiveness and receive it. Once I accepted God's love for
myself, the dam of oppression would lift from my life,
and His love could flow into me, as well as through
me to others.

One of the most amazing aspects of His love was
the fact that even though God knew I would sin again
(sin is, after all, "missing the mark"), He made provisions for all my sins—past, present and future—through
Jesus' death. Wow! What a God! Who but God could
give such love?

Imagining God's capacity for love took awhile for
me to absorb because I based it on my human knowledge of love. If God loved me under all conditions,
then wouldn't it only make sense that when I was
hurting, He was hurting for me? Knowing that God
didn't always like the choices I made but that He still
loved me, was a concept I would have to work on in
order to accept.

Even though God's Word gave me hope and reassurance, my guilt filled me with doubts. Doubts like,
*You'll be an outcast. Everyone will turn against you. God
will never forgive you. Your mother will never forgive you.*

Your baby will be born abnormal as God's punishment.

Where had sin led me? Not only did I have to face the consequences of my mistake, but I must confront my guilt and anxiety. I was thrust into a spiritual battlefield without any armor to protect me. I had to turn my circumstances around and find the courage to face God again. If God could accept me with all my mistakes, surely He could handle my doubts as well.

Once again God showed His faithfulness as I read my Bible verses nightly.

I decided to study God's promises. I only knew a few, but what I did know was powerful enough for me. I eagerly chose my first promise to lean on. God said, "In all things God works for the good of those who love him" (Rom. 8:28).

I must get past the "Why me? Why now?" and stop feeling sorry for myself. It's not as if the answer to either one of these questions would change my situation, so why waste the little energy I had left? I had no alternative but to embrace reality and deal with the consequences of my behavior.

So I kept repeating the scripture *In all things, God works for the good of those who love him.* As I repeated this verse, it was carved it into my heart forever. I recognized later that by putting God's Word in my heart, I stored up God's wisdom and strength. I was claiming God's promises.

I needed a safe, peaceful place where I could think. My church sanctuary became my refuge, my hiding place from the storm that tried to consume me. Only there, I could find the restful peace I needed to clearly see beyond my circumstances. Only there, in God's arms could I seek His gentle guidance to make my decisions.

One important decision was to trust the words I

heard from the pulpit and read in the Bible. I learned that God would receive me just the way I was. But fortunately, He did not want me to stay that way. I came to understand that He wanted more for me than I wanted for myself. He also understood me so much more than I perceived at the time. As time passed, I began to feel His nurturing arms of tender love around me, keeping me safe from the raging storm.

There were no instructions, no "how-to" handbook, specifically addressing crucial decisions for unwed mothers facing an unplanned pregnancy. Surely I wasn't the only person trapped in this dilemma.

I bought a journal and began writing down my feelings, both good and bad. My journal became my secret place to commune with God and my inner self. In my journal I could get in touch with myself and express my deepest thoughts, feelings, and fears. I looked forward to this special time each night before I went to bed to write and rest in my secret place.

I needed to evaluate *my* feelings, so my decisions would be based on what was good for me and my baby, not on what was best for my mother, my father, or the baby's father. After all, my baby's father may or may not be in my baby's future.

I found a tremendous verse one evening as I was reading my Bible. It said, I should accept this challenge (being an unwed mother) as a discipline from the heavenly Father, as a loving gesture. Accept it as something He is doing *for* me, not *to* me—like when my parents told me not to run into the street when I was too young to know the danger that lay ahead. Discipline is most effective when it is followed up with consequences.

My son [daughter], do not make light of the
Lord's discipline, and do not lose heart when
he rebukes you, because the Lord disciplines
those he loves, and he punishes everyone he
accepts as a son [daughter].
—HEBREWS 12:5–6

Well aware that the only two hands large enough to
uphold me in my situation were the Lord's, in His
hands I would rest.

Praise be to the God and Father of our Lord
Jesus Christ, the Father of compassion and
the God of all comfort, who comforts us in
all our troubles, so that we can comfort
those in any trouble with the comfort we
ourselves have received from God.
—1 CORINTHIANS 1:3–4

CHAPTER 5

Walking Through the Alternatives

As a single career woman, what was I going to do with a baby? I lived alone, half a world away from my parents. My job required a great deal of travel. I maintained sixty accounts in a three-state area and worked sixty to seventy hours a week.

It was common knowledge in my department that I was the front-runner for the next corporate sales position. My big break was only months away. I felt confident that once I became a successful sales representative for American Airlines, I could write my own ticket to financial independence. This highly sought-after position represented the kind of security I thought would make me happy. And I certainly would be better off financially than many young women my age who had far more education than I. But now! My security, my future, my hopes, and dreams—all traded for a baby?

At one time I thought of myself as an objective person, but this was not one of those times. My emotions worked overtime to cloud any objectivity. How do you begin to make the biggest decision of your life all alone? Even the word *alone* took on new significance. Living alone didn't bother me, but living alone with a baby sounded like solitary confinement. How do you make the best of a seemingly impossible situation?

While considering the consequences of my choices, I prayed for God's grace as I began thinking through all the alternatives. Thank God, I had somewhere to turn for wisdom and guidance.

> I will instruct you and teach you in the ways you should go; I will counsel you and watch over you.
> —PSALM 32:8

IS ABORTION AN ALTERNATIVE?

Was abortion an alternative I dared consider? Tortured by the thought, but committed to making an informed decision, I began my research. I poured over information from every accessible source. After all, abortion was now legal.

I read about the different types of abortions with caution. Confronting this controversial issue threatened my moral comfort zone. But I had to investigate abortion thoroughly in order to make a responsible, informed decision. If someone was going to do something to my body, I not only wanted to know the complete details of the procedure, I wanted to know all risks and side effects.[1] Besides, not everything that is legal is necessarily moral.

I reflected on growing up in an Irish Catholic family of eleven. The sanctity of life was drilled into my head all of my life. My mother was an example of the commitment to life as she raised nine children. To this day, I admire her unselfish devotion to establish within us a respect for life. It wasn't until now that I realized the sacrifices she endured as she lived by God's choice for life. My mother would be quick to tell you that she did not visualize her life committed to raising children. Her dream was to be a champion figure skater. But her commitment to God's will for her life conquered her own desires.

Under normal circumstances, I believe giving birth is the fulfillment of a God-given nature to reproduce and nurture children. This is part of God's natural order. The blessing of a child authenticates our life. No longer is there a question of worth or purpose for life.

However, I was not dealing with normal circumstances, but with the rude consequences of my choice to be sexually active outside of marriage. I never liked the word "consequences." I didn't like what it implied—living a life of responsible actions, or else.

I must admit I had not seriously thought through the abortion issue until now. But if someone would have asked me for my opinion off the top of my head, I would have said, "It's not for me."

I'm not so sure my decision rested in the fact that I believed an abortion destroys a human life, or if I was just afraid to go through the physical and mental trauma of the actual procedure. However, now I had so much more at stake. I needed a decision I could accept personal responsibility for.

I also realized my decisions affected not only me but also those I loved now and forever. My decision affected the child whose life I now carried, a child who would have no say in this matter. My decision would also affect my future husband if I decided to marry. He would need to be told and be able to live with my decision. Of course, my parents and the baby's father's parents would be denied the privilege of knowing their grandchild, their flesh and blood.

What about my future children? Did they have the right to know there was a sibling they never knew? The more I thought about the rippling effect of this decision, the heavier the burden became. I wondered. If the abortion procedure is so acceptable, why is it so hard to justify or share even with our closest friend?

I began to think about my own conception. How did my mother take the news of pregnancy when she discovered she was pregnant with me? Was I on this earth merely based on a choice my mother made instead of a choice God made? If I truly believed that God is the Creator of life, why did I feel I had a right to change His decision? Did I know more than God? Wasn't this just like the lie the serpent told Eve in the Garden of Eden?

The legal perspective on abortion was just as confusing. Our country was established with the rights of life, liberty, and the pursuit of happiness. In that order. If our most essential "right"—the right to life—is either questioned or denied, does that not open the door for every other right we claim to be scrutinized?

If I am given the freedom to chose between experiencing a nine-month inconvenience or giving my baby life, whose life is above reproach? I was always taught that no personal freedom is rated above human life—anybody's life—no matter the age, color or physical condition. Doesn't the freedom of choice also include the freedom to do what is responsible, as well as right, instead of what is personally or socially convenient?

Conception made me a mother, nothing could reverse that fact, and it was forever. An abortion would not change the fact that I conceived a child, but it would rob me of motherhood, and a child of it's life. Choosing to terminate the life of my child would, of course, bring in the confrontation of more consequences. There's that word again.

Yet there are a few instances where I have questioned the moral issue at hand. For example, when the life of the mother was at stake. If this baby were competing for my life, I would have to say my thought process might be different. I would have to consider the circumstances surrounding my life, like raising other siblings. I would have to pray and seek wise counsel from those who know and love me. I would never have anything but the greatest compassion for any woman who would have to make such an overwhelming decision.

There are also those cases when the mental health of the mother is threatened. Only speaking for myself and my own experiences, I feel that the guilt and physical trauma of an abortion would have been more of a threat to my emotional health than the birth of my unplanned baby.

Only God's love and compassion is consuming enough to encompass these types of decisions. The wisdom and strength to make those choices can only come from the gift of grace through faith. I thank God to this day that I did not belabor this alternative for long. "There, but for the grace of God, go I."[2]

THE ADOPTION OPTION

Adoption has made great strides in the past twenty years. The traditional method of "closed adoption," in which little or no information about biological parents is shared with the adoptive family creates many problems. Now the "open" adoption has become popular for many positive reasons.[3]

Some agencies allow a pregnant woman to choose parents for her child. Agencies offer a selection of profiles on couples waiting for children. In some cases, the birth mother can meet and talk with the prospective parents. This process helps diminish the birth mother's separation grief. It also helps the adopting parents to discuss once mysterious biological heritage of the adopted child.

Although enlightened by the information, thinking about the adoption possibility emotionally overwhelmed me. To me, adoption represented a heart-wrenching alternative in which I was all too familiar. I had witnessed the pain of selfless love through the eyes of my little sister when she was barely sixteen years old. Even though ten years had passed, the traumatic memories lived vividly in my mind. I can still see my sister's face as she lay in her hospital bed only hours after giving birth. When she asked to see her baby the adoption representative said, "I don't think that's a good idea."

"What do you mean!' demanded my sister.

"We feel if you see your child, it would only make the adoption process harder on you."

"I have to! I have to see my baby's face. I have to hold him and tell him how much I love him. I have to tell him I'm sorry I couldn't take him home with me."

"Why don't you take some time to think about it before you decide?" said the lady from the agency.

"I've had nine months to think about it. I have to do what is right for me. I have to see my baby!" demanded my sister.

By this time we were all in tears. No one dared dispute the freedom of her choice. This was a decision she alone would have to live with for the rest of her life. After all, she chose to set aside her own feelings and potential fulfillment through motherhood as she considered the long-term welfare of her child. A selfless sacrifice of this magnitude took a special kind of person. And my little sister, Margie, was special.

Margie made the decision to place her baby for adoption because she realized she was unable to care for a child when she was still a child herself. To this day my little sister is still content with her decision. Margie established a career and is doing well socially and economically. She married a wonderful man and they are looking forward to having children together.

Margie has never forgotten her firstborn son, and on his birthday she takes off work and retreats from the world to pray and think about him. She has two pictures of him that she holds dear—his baby picture and a picture of him on his first birthday. She hopes her son will try to find her someday. And just in case her son inquires about her, she always reports her change of address to the adoption agency.

Years later I finally asked Margie how she got the courage to give her child to strangers. She smiled at me and said, "It didn't take courage; it took grace. Grace is that turbo power that comes from God when we don't have the strength to accomplish something on our own. Besides, the sacrifice I made was not between me and strangers; it was between me and God. I placed my baby in the hands of God. That was the only assurance of my child's ultimate care. God not only gave me the power but He also gave me the peace to live with my decision."

Even in her youth Margie possessed a wisdom

exceeding her years. I doubted my capability for being that special kind of person. I was much too selfish.

Some women have no other alternative, and adoption offers the appropriate and only solution. My heart goes out to them as they face this selfless alternative. They have earned my utmost respect and admiration.

As for me, my heart would not allow me to let go of the only child I may ever have. After all, I was thirty years old, no prospect of marriage in sight, and the possibility of ever bearing another child looked dim. To choose this option I would have to admit an inability to take responsibility for my child, which wasn't the case.

TO SAY "I DO" OR "TOODLE-OO"?

For several months Jim continued to call and check up on me. But his calls became fewer and fewer as he grew tired of talking to my answering machine and leaving messages at work. I felt confident that he was still interested in pursuing our relationship, but would he still be interested if I told him I was pregnant? Did I want him to know I was pregnant? I was so confused I didn't know what to do.

I decided not to think about what he might think or want and concentrate on what was best for me and the new life that I now carried inside.

Would marriage to Jim help me reach my full potential? Would it be worth the sacrifices of home, security, friends, and my new church to marry Jim? The sacrifices might be worth it if we'd experienced mutual love, or if I could see a glimmer of hope for happiness. But should I marry Jim just to give the baby a legitimate name? If Jim agreed to marry me now, would I always wonder if he ever loved me? Would I always be thinking that he married me just to save his career? Were all these legitimate questions, or were my hormones seizing my emotions once more?

I sat there in tears of confusion as I came to realize that all the questions I had asked so far revolved around me and my happiness. Was I selfish for not considering the baby's happiness? On the other hand, I knew that if I wasn't happy, the baby wasn't going to be happy.

The answers to many of these questions were far beyond any wisdom I possessed. So, claiming the promise God gave me in Psalm 32:8, I asked God to help me with my decision.

"O, God help me! Is my selfishness blocking my ability to see the truth? Should I put this precious new life ahead of all my own hopes and dreams? These decisions are too big for me. O good and faithful God, please pull me out of the despair of my sin! Where else can I go but to You? Who else loves me unconditionally? I humble myself before You. Tell me what I should do, and I will do it."

> Whether you turn to the right or to the left, your ears will hear a voice behind you, saying, "This is the way; walk in it."
> —Isaiah 30:21

Recently I had purchased a "Redi-reference," which is a compact biblical guide relating to one hundred topics. I looked up the subject of marriage and found the scriptures on marriage. In these scriptures, God gives a standard by which we can measure the character of a prospective mate. He gives us very specific qualities to look for, and the most important of these is mutual love. God even goes so far as to define love very clearly.

> Love is very patient and kind, never jealous or envious, never boastful or proud, never haughty or selfish or rude. Love does not demand its own way. It is not irritable or touchy. It does not hold grudges and will hardly even notice when others do wrong. It is never glad about injustices, but rejoices whenever truth wins out. If you love someone, you will be loyal to him no matter the cost. You will believe in him, always expect the best of him, and always stand your ground in defending him.
> —1 CORINTHIANS 13:4–7, TLB

By making my decision using God's Word as my guide, I knew I could count on Him throughout this crisis, without Jim.

I carefully scrutinized Jim's character using God's standard for marriage. God revealed His infinite love to me by making my answer crystal clear.

However, Jim was still the father of my baby. What part would I allow him to play in the future of my unborn child? What part would he *want* to play? How would he react to this crisis? Would he even consider this a crisis? How did I want him to react?

So many questions; so little time. All I could do was look up to heaven and ask, "What now?"

My hormones were on a constant roller coaster ride, so maintaining my objectivity remained a constant struggle. Should Jim have input on where we go from here? How much input should fathers have? Should his opinion about how to handle this situation have an impact on my thoughts as well as my decisions?

I truly wanted to believe Jim would consider my best interests and that his motives would be less than self-serving. However, I was sure that I rated, at best, third among his priorities in life. I speculated his career holding the first place position in his life, followed by himself in second place, then possibly me. Was I obligated to listen to what he had to say? Should I consider the options he might offer? I also knew if Jim insisted on his own way, outside of a moral decision, or outside of the decision I made with the Lord's guidance, I would question his motives. I knew the decision rested ultimately between me and God.

Maturity and spiritual growth developed hand in hand, but I had much to learn. My decisions were not always full of wisdom. But God was never long in directing my course.

My job offered me a very stable income with a promising career. There were a lot of single parents who were making it with less than I had.

After much prayer and searching, I decided remaining single was the best alternative for me and my baby. Surely with God's help I could manage.

> Where can I go from your Spirit? Where can I flee from your presence? If I go up to the heavens, you are there: if I make my bed in the depths, you are there. If I rise on the wings of the dawn, if I settle on the far side of the sea, even there your hand will guide me, your right hand will hold me fast.
>
> If I say, "Surely the darkness will hide me and the light become night around me," even the darkness will not be dark to you;

the night will shine like the day, for darkness is as light to you. For you created my inmost being; you knit me together in my mother's womb.

—PSALM 139:7–13

Not only did I decide not to marry Jim, but I decided not to include him in my future at all. I just wouldn't tell him about the pregnancy. I'd tell him not to call anymore. He'd disappear, and my child wouldn't have split loyalties. This way I could protect her from any rejection she might feel from him not choosing to be part of her life. I decided if I never told her father she existed, then she wouldn't have to deal with the harshness of rejection. I was determined to accept full responsibility not only for my child but also for her reactions to this predicament. This would also remove any fear that my child may someday be ripped from my arms and placed in his custody because I allowed him some parental rights.

My heart was in the right place, but my wisdom a little weak. Fortunately, God was still dealing with me slowly and gently. The wisdom of dealing in truth wasn't revealed to me until a few months later.

Still unaware of the pregnancy, Jim made persistent attempts to continue our relationship. I tried to discourage him by explaining the geographical distance between us wouldn't allow a quality relationship, not to mention the fact we hadn't taken time to become good friends before we crossed into sexual relations. Like most relationships today that operate outside of God's intended plan we had only reached the second stage of what I call the three L's—Like, Lust, Love. Stage one is, "I like you. You are friendly, you are visually appealing, you have a gentle spirit, maybe even a nice attitude toward life." Stage two is, "I want you. You look great, I feel a chemistry, I am attracted to you, I desire to touch you." Stage two clouds the mind with fleshly, controlling feelings instead of maintaining a clear head and a pure heart. We become unable to make responsible choices so we fall into stage three which says, "I want to *feel* this good forever." Most relationships never make a solid base in stage three. After falling in love they find it just as easy to stumble out.

I believe that God's plan goes like this: Stage one stays the same, "I like you. You are friendly, you are visually appealing, you have a gentle spirit, maybe even a nice attitude toward life." But stage two is reached with the marriage covenant, "I love the person you are. I choose to make you a part of the rest of my life, not because of what I feel but because I value you and I am committed to making this relationship work." Stage three is reached through patient anticipation and self-denial. It proves God's faithfulness to those who love Him and keep His commandments, "I want you and only you forever. You look great, and you are mine. I choose to have you. I desire to possess you as a sacred treasure."

I had disturbed the natural order of God's plan. I discovered sexual activity produced a bond between Jim and I that unfortunately didn't end with the relationship. Even if I had not conceived a baby, the bond of intimacy was still there. Like other men I'd had intimate relations with, it created a soul tie that could haunt me at Satan's will.

I read that, "Physical sexual intimacy, instead of being just one more building block within the structure of a relationship, actually expresses that relationship's completion. It is the capstone of a relationship, the fulfillment of intimacy. When a man and woman engage in physical sexual intimacy, they are expressing wholeness, oneness."[4] Every time I gave myself to someone, I gave a part of myself away.

In a mutually committed relationship there is a completeness achieved when the constant circle of giving and receiving is maintained. The circle grows bigger as children are then brought into the circle. If or when this mutual cycle of giving and receiving stops, the circle becomes incomplete, exposed, vulnerable. Once the circle has been ruptured, it takes time and the healing power of God to fully recover and begin again.

CHAPTER 6

God's Visitor at My Front Door

The weekend had finally arrived. I was exhausted. My job presented its own set of challenges, but my body was housing an emotional marathon. I couldn't wait to get home and lock myself away. The moment the clock struck 5 P.M. I packed up my briefcase and headed for the door. Several friends shared their weekend plans and various invitations were extended, but nothing sounded as good as being home alone.

On the way home I stopped for a take-out dinner and headed for my personal oasis. As I walked through my apartment door, I breathed a sigh of relief. I dropped everything and slipped off my shoes. I laid across my bed for what I thought would be my traditional ten-minute power nap and woke up two hours later.

I heated up my cold dinner and listened to my phone messages. Carmen had called three times to confirm our breakfast meeting time. I had totally forgotten that I had agreed to meet her for breakfast

Saturday morning to talk about moving in together. Weeks ago she had generously invited me to move in with her, but this was before I knew I was pregnant. Now with two for the price of one, I felt she would certainly reconsider. We needed to talk.

I called Carmen and asked her if she would mind coming over to my place for breakfast. I really didn't feel like going out anywhere. She graciously agreed.

The next morning, Carmen, totally unaware of my agenda, arrived all excited with ideas about how to arrange her three bedroom house, which room I would share, new paint for the bathroom, and wallpaper for the dining room—and on and on. I let her talk as I finished cooking breakfast and gathering my courage. The aroma of crisply cooked bacon filled the room. Now breakfast was ready, and we sat down to eat while the coffee finished perking.

"You're awful quiet this morning. Are you feeling OK?" Carmen asked.

"I'm OK. I just have a lot on my mind. Carmen, I know that I said I thought moving in with you might be a good idea, but something has come up," I said, as tears began to well up in my eyes.

"What? What is it?" she asked tenderly. I couldn't hold it any longer. I spewed out the words.

"I'm pregnant!"

My usually verbose friend sat there expressionless. I kept on talking for fear she would leave before the coffee was perked. "I understand your spiritual convictions, Carmen, and I wouldn't blame you if you no longer want me to move in with you. It wouldn't be a good witness for me to be seen going in and out of your house with my sin, big as life, right out in front of me. I don't want people thinking you're endorsing premarital sex."

Carmen slowly scooted her chair back, and I thought, *She's leaving.* But I should have known her better than that. She got up and came over and hugged me.

"Deb, I am so excited for you!"

Excited? Well there was a reaction I had not expected. Could she have misunderstood me? *Oh please, don't make me say it again.* In a heartbeat she switched from painting and papering *our* stuff to talking about how we could fix up the third bedroom for the baby. *Baby!* There was another word I was not quite used to yet.

Carmen was thirty-four and had been single all of her life. So I sat in awe when she said very lovingly, "Deb, I have always wanted to have children. Maybe this is the Lord's way of providing for me vicariously."

What was she saying? Was she offering to be an integral part of my pain and joy? How could she sort out all the bare facts to see the blessing?

Once the bomb was dropped, she was not the least shell-shocked, but came out of the foray asking a lot of questions.

What a relief! I had been longing to share with someone whom I could trust. So, I filled her in on all the details and asked her to keep it confidential. I wasn't quite ready for the public "stoning." I shared with Carmen my fears, which were basically, What would people think?

Carmen smiled broadly and said, "Deb, you will be surprised at how people react." She was certainly right so far. Carmen was my first living example of God's love and forgiveness.

After several hours of sharing and caring, Carmen got quiet. I could tell she was choosing her words carefully before she spoke.

"Deb, do you know that God is with you, even now?"

I hung my head. I found it very hard to think about facing God right now. Though He may not have walked away from me, I felt sure He had His back to me. And that was OK; that is what I deserved. Besides, I was afraid to look into His face and see His disappointment. At this point, I wasn't emotionally strong enough to deal with that heavy load.

After one hundred years of silence, I said, "I sincerely doubt that God is on speaking terms with me right now."

"I think you're wrong. It's in our weakest moments that we become His favorites. I realize that's probably hard for you to understand, but I know someone who can explain it better than I can."

"Carmen, I appreciate your concern, but I'm still trying to sort things out in my own mind before I go public."

"But couldn't you use some wise counsel in figuring things out?" she asked.

"Right now I'd listen to just about anybody who could make sense, but I'm not quite ready to share my sin with the world."

"What if I went with you and spoke for you? Would that help?" she asked with such compassion. "Deb, I hate to be so insistent, but I truly believe, with all my heart, that this is the right thing, at the right time. I want you to speak to Pastor George."

"You want me to do what?"

"It's biblical to go to the elders of the church and confess our sin, so that we might be set free and receive their wisdom."

Our church had over three thousand members. Somehow, even telling my mother sounded easier. I said, "I have a better idea. I'll just brand my forehead with a scarlet 'S' and be done with it."

Carmen exploded in laughter. Finally she said, "Debi, that's what the Bible says to do. Just pray about it, and if you change your mind and want to go, I'll go with you."

A few weeks later, I called the church and made an appointment to see Pastor George. They set the date for the very next day. I was so relieved that I didn't have to agonize over this any longer than that. It helped me so much to know that I had moral support in Carmen. The few hours before the next day seemed interminable.

Finally the dawn came. We arrived early. I knew this wasn't the time for small talk. As soon as I hit the chair in the Pastor's office, I choked out the words, "Pastor, I'm pregnant." His compassionate expression didn't change. He simply said, "I knew that before you came Deborah. The Holy Spirit revealed it to me right after you made your appointment."

I sat there speechless. Pastor George was gracious and sympathetic. He asked, "What are your plans, Deborah?"

"Well, I've decided to raise my baby alone, and Carmen has offered me a place to live. I would like to continue coming to church here, but I will drop out of the singles group before anyone learns I'm pregnant. I realize I would represent a bad testimony for this church's single community. I don't want to be a bad influence. . ."

"Deborah, I want you to wait before you make the decision to drop out. Pray about it. If you still feel strongly about dropping out, then I'll understand your decision."

He then encouraged me to share my crisis with a

few close Christians friends to start the disclosure process. He also advised me the importance of receiving love and support from members of the church family.

As we concluded the visit, my pastor said, "Deborah, my door is always open to you. If you need anything, please come and see me."

Up to this point in my life, I couldn't even imagine what it would be like to commune with our heavenly Father. But after this visit with my pastor, I felt as though some of that mystery had been unveiled.

It was hard to get to sleep that night, and so I just lay there, thinking about what was ahead of me. My whole rededication to the Lord seemed to be a farce at this point. The mere thought of it made me weak. I knew with my own strength alone I would never be brave enough to face this kind of humility. On the one hand I was longing to be free of the secret that imprisoned me. On the other hand my fear of rejection was more than I could stand right now.

OH, HOLY NIGHT!

Later that month, at the singles Christmas party, everyone was asked to stand and tell what the singles group meant to them. I froze in my chair. Up until now the only three people in the room who knew I was pregnant were Carmen, Tom, and the singles pastor, who just happened to be seated in front of me. Had the Lord provided this opportunity to set me free from the bondage of secrecy? I prayed for strength as person after person shared their story. Periodically, I glanced at the pastor. He just smiled at me with a reassuring smile. If now was the time, I wanted to appear confident. I needed to be a good witness to others so they knew that I was trusting God to carry me through this.

Finally I stood up. The silence screamed at me to run. Only the grace of God held me there. Summoning up every ounce of courage I had, I explained, "I came to this singles group more than five months ago, skeptical, but seeking. I experienced kind faces and gentle spirits everywhere. But past experience told me unexplained kindness came with a price tag. *Surely they wanted something*, were the cynical words running through my suspicious mind. Time showed me differently.

"As I grew spiritually, I understood the giving nature of Christians. Unconditional giving was foreign to my hardened heart. But through my association with this church and this singles group, I learned that love is not a feeling but a commitment."

Seeing the love and compassion in their faces, I had courage to continue. "I have come to rely on this class for support and nurturing because my family lives five hundred miles away. You've become my family, and I hope I can count on your continued support in the future . . . because I am expecting a baby in June."

I quickly sat down. A flood of tears poured from my eyes. Why was I crying? They weren't tears of shame or humility. Surely I had done the right thing at the right time. Inside, I knew these were tears of joy and relief as I celebrated the freedom I felt at that moment.

The truth will set you free.

—JOHN 8:32

The party ended in prayer, and a flood of people came to hug me and share similar or related experiences from their lives. Making myself vulnerable allowed others the freedom to open their mental dark closets and share their past hurts.

Although the singles had so warmly embraced me, I wasn't foolish enough to think I could get through this crisis without God's divine strength and protection. I needed this extension of God's grace and forgiveness and to be involved with other Christians where I could grow and learn about our merciful Father. Attending church helped me battle all the negative emotions flooding my mind. Even though I felt unworthy of God's, or anyone else's love, I felt at peace.

It was quite a revelation to me to finally realize that, more than money, I wanted what money could not buy. I wanted joy and peace, and I wanted to know and associate with those who had it. God allowed me to know Him more and more through those He strategically placed in my life. In some of my darkest moments, I can still recall how the Lord revealed His love for me through others.

Late in my pregnancy, I sat in church on Sunday morning, trying to gather my spiritual strength to face another week. One of my new friends from our singles class approached me. He stood there rather shyly and said, "As I was praying last night, the Lord brought you to my mind. Please accept this in Christian love." And he handed me an envelope.

"Thank you for your kindness," was all I could say. I was dying of curiosity but not wanting to embarrass him, I kept the envelope in my Bible until I got home. Without taking off my coat, I sat down, tore the envelope open and read:

Deborah,

God's Visitor at My Front Door

You are, indeed, a woman of great courage to under-take this unfortunate circumstance alone. You will be a testimony to others who witness your faithful walk. As the Lord brought you to my mind, He gave me this poem for you.

In God's love,
Mike

> God's plans for thee are graciously unfolding,
>   And leaf by leaf they blossom perfectly,
>   As yon fair rose, from its soft enfolding,
>   In marvelous beauty opens fragrantly.
>   Oh, wait in patience for the dear Lord's coming,
>   For sure deliverance He'll bring to thee;
>   Then, how thou shalt rejoice at the fair dawning
>   Of what sweet morn which ends thy long captivity.

The singles class constantly showed their support as they helped me move into Carmen's house and fix up the nursery. All through my pregnancy, I had more friends and more love to share than I ever could have imagined. I knew Jesus loved me today, tomorrow, and forever. God does indeed work in unexpected and wonderful ways.

> Trust in the Lord with all your heart and lean not on your own understanding; in all your ways acknowledge him, and he will make your paths straight.
> —PROVERBS 3:5–6

As my love for the Lord grew, so did my faith. I just

kept telling myself, *I can do all things through Christ who strengthens me* (Philippians 4:13). These were God's promises. I held them close to my heart. I would not forget them.

> I tell you the truth, if you have faith as small as a mustard seed, you can say to this mountain, "Move from here to there" and it will move, nothing will be impossible for you.
> —MATTHEW 17:20–21

A WAY OUT?

One Sunday morning after church Tom approached me. Good ol' Tom, who had been my neighbor before I moved in with Carmen. Smiling sweetly, he said, "Deborah, would you have lunch with me?"

I didn't think anything about it. It was not unusual for the singles to gather and agree to meet at a specified place for lunch. Tom often spearheaded the effort. And Tom, much like Carmen, took it upon himself to be my self-appointed guardian angel.

"Let me ask Carmen if she wants to come?" I automatically responded.

"Wait!" Tom said. "I'd rather you didn't." Tom looked at me with an unusually serious face and said, "I really wanted just you this time, if you don't mind? I really want to talk to you alone."

"OK, but I'll have to make some arrangements with Carmen. We came together in my car."

Tom said. "Just let her take your car, and I'll bring you home after lunch."

My curiosity stirred. What could Tom possibly have to say to me that he couldn't say in front of Carmen. *He sounds serious*, I thought. This surprising display of seriousness appeared quite out of character for Tom. He was better known for his corny wit than his sobriety.

I told Carmen I was going with Tom for lunch.

Immediately she asked, "Where shall I meet you?"

"Not this time. He sounds like he has something serious to discuss with me only."

"What?" she asked surprised.

"I don't know."

Carmen's face showed her disapproval of being left in the dark about anything, especially when it pertained to me. She walked a fine line between influencing my life and controlling my life. But still, I held the greatest respect for her, as well as her unsolicited opinions. I didn't mind at all having her as my "guardian angel."

"Carmen, please don't worry about me. I'm a big girl. And if it will make you feel better I do hereby promise not to do anything foolish or irresponsible in the next two to three hours."

"I'm not worried about *you*. It's *Tom* I'm concerned about."

"Carmen! How can you say that? This is good ol' Tom we're talking about. If you'll remember correctly, it was Tom's encouragement that kept me coming back to this church. He's a good friend and a gentleman, and better than that, he's a Christian gentleman."

"Deborah, being a Christian doesn't make you perfect. Tom's still a man."

"OK, Mom, I'll be sure to let you know when I get home," I said, shaking my head as I walked over to meet Tom who had been patiently waiting by the door.

It felt good to have someone open the car door for

me and take my arm to help me in. It had been so long since I had dated. I'd forgotten what it felt like to be catered to. Tom was always the perfect gentleman. Even if a lady was riding in the back seat of his car, he would be there to help with her door. I imagined he acted the same way with his mother. I could see him as the perfect son. His etiquette complimented his personality of gentleness and compassion.

"Where are we going?" I asked, as we drove away.

"That depends on you. How long can I have your attention?"

"I don't have anything planned until six o'clock."

"Great," he beamed.

"However," I cautioned, "I would like to be back for church tonight. It takes both services on Sunday to keep my spirits up enough to make it till Wednesday night's service."

"You are handling this whole ordeal with grace and dignity," he assured me.

"Well, there's a lot of pressure at work, and I still haven't told them yet."

"You haven't told anyone at work?" Tom asked in surprise.

"I just can't seem to find the right words or the appropriate time. I never realized how hard those two words are to say. I'd almost rather announce it at our staff meeting and watch the gossip fly. That kind of news goes through the office like wildfire."

"You haven't told *anyone*?"

"Just my friend Marla. I had to tell her. We went on a business trip together last week, and after the second time I had her pull the car over—I couldn't keep down my breakfast. She became a little concerned, so I confessed."

"How did she take it?"

"She was great. She even started pampering me."

But when I told Cassie, she looked at me in total shock. She asked, "What are you going to do?" as if my life had just ended. Fortunately, I had already worked through that phase, so I said, 'I'm taking it day by day with God, and good friends helping me.' I think she was more amazed at my attitude than my pregnancy."

"You *are* quite amazing," Tom said unexpectedly.

Trying to conceal my red face, I asked, "Why would you say that? 'Amazing' is hardly a word that fits my description right now."

"I'm amazed when I see how much you've grown spiritually in these past four months."

"Well, now you'll be able to watch my stomach grow along with my spirit," I said jokingly.

"I'm serious, Debi. I wish you could see yourself through my eyes. Here you are, a baby Christian, and you are facing these tremendous spiritual challenges so bravely. You are walking out your faith. You are a living testimony to everyone around you."

"Tom, you've got it all wrong. I'm facing these tremendous spiritual challenges because of the consequences of my sin. The words 'you are a sinner' have taken on a new meaning. Not only do I feel like a sinner mentally, but now I get to wear my sin physically; and my morning sickness has put a new twist on what it feels like to be a sinner. For the past several years I've walked around with my head up so high I couldn't even see God. So any grace you see is the unmerited gift of God's grace that is freely given to any sinner."

Tom looked at me with a gentle smile. "I believe what your saying is true, but I'm concerned that you are too hard on yourself. It's true that you are a sinner, but we are all sinners. It says in Romans 3:23, *for all have sinned and fall short of the glory of God.* But before we were sinners, we were created in the image of God. Deborah, I just want you to learn to see the special person that God has created you to be."

"Well, to tell you the truth, Tom, special is not one of the feelings I've been experiencing lately."

"That will change as you stay close to the Lord," Tom said, as he pulled into the parking lot of the Anatole Hotel.

"What are we doing here?" I asked rather abruptly.

"They serve a wonderful brunch buffet. I thought I'd take you somewhere special."

"Thanks for thinking of it." I couldn't bring myself to tell him that this is where I first met Jim. "But what's the special occasion?"

"I'll tell you over dessert," he said with a sheepish grin.

As Tom and I sat and chatted through breakfast, I caught myself drifting off into the memories of the day I met Jim. *If only I could have known what would come of that flirtatious afternoon. If only I would have followed my first instincts and continued to thwart his persistent advances. If only, if only, if only.*

"Deborah, are you OK?"

"No! We have to get out of here or I'll never hear a word you say."

"What's the matter?"

"I'll tell you when we get to the car. I'm sorry to ruin this lovely brunch, but I just can't stay here any longer."

Tom quickly paid the bill, and we left the hotel. When we got to the car, he took my hand and asked, "Are you OK?"

"I'll be fine. I should have been honest with you before we went in, and this wouldn't have happened."

"What? What happened?"

"This is the hotel where the Republican Convention was held where I met Jim," I said in a low voice.

"I'm so sorry! I didn't even think about that. I am so sorry!"

"No, Tom, it's not your fault. I should have handled it better. I shouldn't have gone in. I should never have gone into that stupid hotel in the first place." I couldn't stop my tears.

Tom pulled me close to him and let me cry on his shoulder. I could hear him praying softly. He reached into his pocket and pulled out a white cotton handkerchief.

"A handkerchief?" I asked in surprised.

"That's all I have, but it's clean," he said apologetically.

"Oh no, I'm not complaining. It's just that this reminds me of my dad. He use to always carry this same kind of white cotton handkerchief with him wherever he went. How well I remember ironing them when I was a little girl."

"I guess that puts me in the old-fashioned category," he said.

"Not really. It just reminds me that it's been a long time since my dad's handkerchief dried my tears."

"Maybe it's time for a trip home," Tom said softly.

"My father doesn't know I'm pregnant."

"There's plenty of time for that."

We were halfway home before I realized that Tom had not told me the reason he had asked me to lunch. "By the way, what did you want to talk about?" I questioned.

"It can wait."

"No, I really want to know. It's obviously important

for you to go to so much trouble."

"I just want to help you through this."

"You are, Tom. You've been very supportive and a great friend."

"That's easy, Deborah. You bring out the best in me."

Then, taking a deep breath, he said, "Deb, there is something I want you to think about. You don't have to respond today. I've given this idea a great deal of thought, and I hope you will too."

"What is it, Tom? You know I have a great deal of respect for your opinions."

Tom started very hesitantly, "What if . . . what if . . ." and he hesitated again. Then, seeming to regain his courage, he said quickly, "What if you and I were to get married? I could claim the baby to be mine and no one would have to know the difference. I'm not perfect, but I think I'd make a good father. And God knows I'd try to be a good husband to you."

He caught me totally off guard. I sat there just staring at him. What could I say? Tears freely coursed down my cheeks. Finally, I said, "Tom, you are so sweet. What a sensitive thing to do," I said as I began to cry again. "Here you are, willing to give up your reputation for me."

"Trust me. It's not that great a sacrifice. I'm afraid you may end up with the short end of the stick, so to speak."

"I don't know what to say." By that time we had pulled up to the front of my home.

"Don't say anything," he said. And then looking me straight in the eye, he said, "Deb, you have to know that I care for you a great deal. I'm *not* just trying to be nice. Just think about it, and call me."

Before he could help me out of the car, I jumped

out, assuring him I would think about it. Then I said, "Good-bye, Tom, and thank you so much for caring."

"Call me," he repeated. I waved an OK as I turned to go in. I felt sure Carmen would be waiting at the door, dying to know what Tom had said.

Sure enough, there she was. "Hi," I said, as I went to my bedroom to change clothes.

Predictably, she followed me in and sat down on my bed.

"Where did you go for lunch?"

"The Anatole."

"The Anatole! What was the occasion?"

"He said he thought I was special."

"Did you tell him that you didn't think the Anatole was so special?"

"Eventually."

"Come on out with it. What is he up to? In all the years I've known Tom he has never taken anyone to the Anatole."

"He asked me to marry him."

"He what? No! You're kidding me!"

"No."

"No, he didn't ask you to marry him, or no, you aren't kidding me?"

"Yes, he asked me to marry him, and no, I'm not kidding you."

"Why would he do that?" she asked.

"He wants to protect my reputation. He wants to get married right away and let everyone assume the baby is his."

"But that's not so!"

"I thought it was noble of him," I said defensively.

"Well, I see it as an act of desperation. Everyone knows he has a thing for you, and this is a desperate act to accomplish a selfish goal."

"Back off, Carmen. This is not your concern."

There was a long silence. Carmen got up and gave me a hug.

"You're right. I know you'll do the right thing."

Of course I knew she was right, but I wasn't about to tell her that. She never mentioned it again, nor did I.

I was well aware that the only way to get through my trial was to listen to God's word and stand on the truth. I already knew in my heart that a marriage at this time wouldn't work.

PROFITABILITY OR INTEGRITY?

Three months pregnant, and my secret was still safe at work. However, time was becoming my enemy. Everyday as I walked into the office, I would say, "Not yet, not yet!" I needed more time to prepare myself for the varied responses I would inevitably receive. But God saw it differently.

I walked into the office Monday morning after a long week of traveling. My supervisor met me at the door with a big smile on his face. The guilt I carried with my secret told me, "He knows!"

"Congratulations!" he said, shaking my hand. Surely he could see the fire in my cheeks. "I'm proud of you. It's nice to know that some people get what they deserve."

"Thanks, but what do you think I deserve?"

"Mr. Evans is waiting for you in his office. I told him I'd send you over to the sales office as soon as you arrived."

I felt my heart beating through my chest. I walked into the sales manager's office. Mr. Evans got up from his desk and came around to shake my hand.

"Congratulations, you're now part of our sales team! It's a lot of responsibility and hard work but you've proved you can do it. Welcome to the family."

Those words were like music to my ears. The job I had been working toward for five years was mine for the taking. I had finally reached my goal. What now?

Yet I just sat there, drowning in a sea of emotions. I wanted to jump up and shout. Instead, I found myself asking, *God, why now?*

The long silence was broken when the sales manager noticed my reluctance. "What's the problem?" he asked.

I knew what I was about to say would start an avalanche of events that would be out of my control. Yet, I knew I had to face this situation head on. As I began to speak, I felt a warmth rise up within me and a confidence that I couldn't explain, except for the presence of God. My words came surely and calmly as I presented my situation.

I've never seen anyone's facial expression change so dramatically, so quickly. Mr. Evans knew how hard I'd worked for this job.

After several uneasy moments, I said, "Sir, I hope you know that I consider this offer a great compliment, and I want more than anything to accept this position. However, my life is going in a new direction, and I feel I need to honor this new commitment."

It was not hard to read his body language, so I didn't keep him in suspense. I said forthrightly, "I am carrying a child, and I need to adjust my priorities."

He sat there trying to look composed, and I sat there trying not to cry.

I continued, "I don't think, as a single mother, I would be a good representative for the image of this company."

As he fished for something to say, I could only imagine his thoughts—especially since he knew I had dated his boss a time or two.

Finally, in a very professional, but kindly tone, he asked, "Is there anything I can do?"

"Yes," I answered quickly. "I would appreciate it if our conversation was kept confidential for a few more weeks."

"I understand," he agreed. "You can count on it."

And then he asked, obviously still overwhelmed by the situation, "Why did you reveal your pregnancy? You know, you could have accepted the position, and no one would have been able to do anything about it. You could have had everything you've worked for."

I smiled and said, "There was a time when I would have done just that. But I have found a new church, and I'm working on a new way of life."

He stood there looking a little confused, but pleased. Then he confided in me that he too, was a Christian and understood my stand. Perhaps he was even more aware of the rewards that would eventually follow my stand.

He then shared with me that his wife was very knowledgeable about our company's insurance coverage and maternity benefits, and he invited me to his home for dinner to meet his wife and their two children.

I accepted his invitation, and later I met his wife, Sue, and their children. She had prepared a lovely meal. After dinner, Sam discretely took the children and left us alone to talk in the kitchen. Their home had a peaceful quality. Sue's personality resembled my older sister's. She put me at ease as I talked, and she listened intently.

I left their home that night feeling whole and peaceful. God had so graciously allowed our paths to cross. Sam and Sue provided a living testimony to me of a solid Christian family, willing to help and bless my life.

TRUTH REMOVES THE SHACKLES OF SIN

The days became a series of emotional highs followed by frequent lows of shame and remorse. I was at my strongest early in the day, but by nighttime, I would become vulnerable and weak as my body began to fatigue. Doubts would visit me regularly to steal my peace and plague my rest. I'd spend hours searching for answers to seemingly unanswerable questions. One night out of sheer exhaustion, I humbly placed myself at the feet of our merciful heavenly Father with this prayer.

> "Tell me, Father, where do I begin? I really want to go the way You would have me go and say what You would have me say. I'm lost in the dark. As I reach out, I feel nothing but paralyzing fear. I can't even find the walls of my self-made prison. There are no boundaries or rules in this merciless game of strife. Help me find my way. Help me find the light switch that exposes my enemies and reveals Your truth."

I opened my Bible in search for the truth that would set me free. I'd tried reading the Bible before. While some of it made sense, other parts just flew somewhere way above my head. I learned that knowledge is acquired, and wisdom is a gift from God. I needed the wisdom that comes through the Holy Spirit to understand and decipher the Word of God.

Jesus answered, "I am the way and the truth and the life."

—JOHN 14:6

For the next several months, I read a lot of self-help books. I read books on the birthing process and parenting. I read anything I could put my hands on to give me confidence.

As I searched, bits and pieces of wisdom surfaced, and I thought back on my decision not to inform Jim of my pregnancy. To keep the truth from him would set me up for a lifetime of dishonesty. That decision could leave me fearful that at any moment my lies would be discovered and my credibility destroyed. I wanted, to live free from fear, so I knew I had to make that dreaded call and expose my secret.

It had been several months since my last conversation with Jim. I was more than three months pregnant when he called, and not knowing my "condition," he begged me to come to Washington, D.C., to see him inaugurated into his new term of office as state representative. The offer was tempting. I thought about showing up and surprising him with "Oh, by the way!" But I decided to stay home and save myself any more grief. Instead, I made it clear that I was not interested in continuing our relationship.

So as I picked up the phone and dialed the number, now two months later, I silently prayed, *O Lord, give me strength and dignity.* I hoped he wasn't at home. This wasn't the kind of message one leaves on the answering machine.

He answered the phone.

"Jim, this is Deborah. . . ."

Before I could continue he said, "Hi, what are you up to these days?"

"Jim, I have something important to tell you."

"OK, what is it?"

"I thought you should know you're going to be a father in June."

There was silence for what seemed to feel like about one hundred years. Then at last he said, "I'm sorry."

"Well, it takes two to make a baby," I said emphatically.

Jim shot back, "I don't suppose you want to get married?"

I was hardly complimented by such an attractive proposal. I am sure my response was a great relief to him.

"We barely know each other."

"Then what **do** you want?" he asked abruptly. The cheer had gone from his voice.

"I wanted you to know about the baby so that you may decide what part you want to play in your child's life."

Silence.

"At first, I was not going to tell you, but then I realized the only way to get through this situation with any peace was to handle it with the cold, hard truth."

"Well, thanks for calling," and the line went dead.

Feeling numb, relieved, and rejected, I knew I had done the right thing. Then I began to reason in my mind, *Jim needs time to think through the news. This crisis was not mine alone even though up until now it sure felt like it. I shouldn't judge his first reaction. It may not be a clue about his ultimate decision. Jim must decide how and if he would participate in the baby's life as well as consider the lifelong implications of his decision.*

Adjustments were a constant process for me during this time. The physical adjustments were hard enough, but the mental adjustments left me even more exhausted. There were many days filled with embarrassment and confusion as the eyes of my world stared at me.

I remember one evening in particular. Carmen and I were invited to a baby shower for Natalie, a lady who attended our church. We went to a local department store and picked out the perfect gift for her baby. And Carmen urged me to buy a few things that were on sale for my baby. She was so excited as she rummaged through the sales rack, ooohing and giggling with delight.

"Look at this!" she would say. "Oh, look how precious!"

For the first time, I looked at this life I was carrying as precious. I decided it was time to celebrate. So I heartily joined with Carmen as we began a trousseau for *my baby*.

We arrived at the shower a little late. We had celebrated in the baby department a little too long. We walked in, still giggling from our adventure. Carmen opened the door for me. As I stood in the middle of the door, the whole room went suddenly silent. I felt everyone's eyes on me. Carmen came immediately to the rescue.

"Hi, guys. Sorry we're late. We were having so much fun in the baby department we lost track of time."

The chatter began again, and the party was back in full swing.

The rest of the evening went fairly smooth, but even with friends to share my pain, I still felt lost and alone.

I know now that I was on an emotional roller coaster of feelings, some caused by guilt and loneliness, others caused by hormonal changes. Facing each emotion and physical change was a constant battle.

When would this nightmare end?

I opened my journal that night and poured my heart onto its pages.

Dear God,

Tonight my eyes flood with tears. Where are they coming from? My weak and frail self is creeping through again, trying to regain control of my life. I feel exposed and vulnerable. I want to find a dark corner to hide from this world until I can rest and restore my strength.

I have always been a very private person. Now my life is an open book for the world to critique. I hurt. I feel awkward and misplaced. I see pity and sympathy in the eyes of those who dare to look at me. It is as though I carried a disease, instead of the miracle of life.

I don't want anyone to feel sorry for me. Lord, I want to be happy and full of the joy You promise. What good does it do to feel peace within if I am constantly dealing with turmoil? I have always been a strong person, a comforter and "consoler," the giver—not the receiver. Now I am faced with a role that is foreign to me, and I am lost in humiliation. I sincerely pray You have control of my life, Lord, because I do not.

I face each day confused and searching. My strength is drained. I have been defeated by circumstances. O Lord, take the wheel of my life and gently guide me down the scenic roads; the expressways have become too fast for me.

Prayerfully, Your child,
Deborah

Although I went to bed that night with a heavy heart, the Lord answered my prayers and renewed my strength and peace of mind. I awoke the next morning with an unexpected, unexplainable grateful heart. My thoughts were of a merciful God. A God who was allowing me to receive His gifts of wisdom, humility, and perseverance, while living through the consequence of my sin. That night God gave me a glimpse of the big picture He was painting for my life.

CHAPTER 7

Letting Go of the Past, Holding on to Love

*L*ast experiences are a great resource for analyzing today's behavior—both the good and the bad. As children we learn to react to events by observing the people closest to us. They teach us how to respond to other people and events until we are old enough to make decisions of our own. Learning comes not only by spoken word, but even more influential are the actions behind the words spoken. Growing up in a dysfunctional family provided me a wealth of experiences to work through and evaluate as an adult. It didn't take long to learn that reprogramming old unhealthy responses would be hard work.

Through the suggestion of a counselor, I read a life-changing book called *The Bruises of Satan*, by Carroll Thompson. This book opened my eyes to many mysteries involving past hurts. While my thoughts and feelings concerning my past were justifiable, it also told me I was unhealthy to hold on to my pain as an adult.

The most helpful point in this book explains how we transfer the relationship we have with our earthly fathers to the relationship we have with our heavenly Father. "One's relationship to the heavenly Father is built upon the relationship to one's earthly father. Those who grow up feeling a father's rejection have nothing upon which to build a spiritual relationship with God. They tend to see the heavenly Father in the same way they view their earthly father. It takes time and truth for them to look to God as their Father."[5]

In my case, I viewed God like my dad—in the distance and too busy to look at me individually. I was just one of nine needy children.

"Giving time and giving of self are necessary to communicate love."[6] As a child there were days when I felt angry about the lack of individual attention I received. But it wasn't until I grew to be an adult that I discovered I still harbored unforgiveness in my heart toward my father. Much to my surprise I also find myself guilty of using my father to catch the blame for my desire to be intimately held by a man. *If Dad would have only held me and loved me as a child, I wouldn't have these wounds in my spirit. I wouldn't have this craving to be wanted and feel loved by a male substitute*, I said time and time again.

However, time and maturity told me that being an adult meant growing up and taking responsibility for my actions. "The unforgiving mind sees itself as innocent and others as guilty. It thrives on conflict and on being right, and it sees inner peace as its enemy."[7] Some of my inner wounds were so deep that in order to begin my journey to healing and wholeness, I had to start by forgiving one person at a time beginning with my dad. I had to make the choice to live miserably in the past or forgive and get on with the inner peace that God promises. I alone held the power to be pitiful or powerful. So I began to pray for God to show me the way to forgive and forget.

One day after church, my friend Natalie, a new found friend from our singles class, paid me a visit. In spite of her fiery red hair, Natalie had a gentle way about her.

"I thought about you in church today. How are you doing?"

"It's funny you should ask, Natalie. Today I'm struggling, but I'm not quite sure with what. On one hand I think it's how to love and then on the other hand I think it's how to forgive. The more I think about it, the more confused I become. Just when I seem to take two steps up the mountain of under-standing, then I take one step back. I know I've come a long way, but the summit seems so far away."

"I know, Deborah; I've always found when I'm climbing a mountain, it's better not to look up or down, but at the next step."

"That sounds good, Natalie, but it's not easy."

"Deborah, just try to tell me how you feel."

"Well, I use to think I was a pretty nice person, but the more I learn about Jesus, the worse I feel about myself. And now I discover that I've got to get to know Jesus even more to find the love of God the Father. But how do I find real love when I'm not sure what it looks like, and now, all of a sudden, I no longer feel like I deserve it?

However, deciding to seek a close and trusting rela-tionship with God presents another problem for me. You see, God is a man, or at least He represents a man, and up to this point in my life, every man I ever loved or cared about has abused or disappointed me. My wounds are deep, and the fear of giving or receiving love from any man is a rather scary proposition.

Natalie looked at me with such compassion and gently grabbed my hand and led me to the sofa. "Did you know that forgiveness and love often work together. You can't have one without the other. So maybe you need to work through forgiveness and heal some past wounds in order to be free to experience love. I think your pregnancy is merely a consequence of a bigger unresolved problem. Deborah, I see so many of the same voids in your life that I experienced in my own. I see the same inward desire to fulfill an aching emptiness left from a lack of intimacy growing up. Tell me about your relationship with your father."

"With nine children, my father's time was consumed with financial responsibilities and emotional wounds. When he wasn't working to make ends meet he was numbing his own emotional wounds at the local tavern. My father didn't know how to show love. He was a strong disciplinarian with my six brothers. His father had taught him how to instill fear, which he passed on to his sons. But my father didn't have a clue as to what to do when a little blue-eyed girl crawled up into his lap and hugged his neck and melted his heart. I constantly felt put aside. There were so many questions I wanted to ask my dad. I often wondered what and who he saw when he looked at me.

It wasn't until I was a teenager that I made a painful observation about fathers. One day after school I went home with my friend Cherrie to study for a history exam. I sat in amazement when Cherrie's Dad sat down with us and asked about the activities of our day at school. Her father listened intently and even asked questions which, to me, showed his real interest. It wasn't until I watched Cherrie's father pick her up and swing her around, saying, "I love you," that I began to hurt deep inside. I sat speechless in the distance, feeling robbed of the intimacy of a father-daughter relationship. I felt sure that my father loved me, or at least he cared what happened to me. But my father had no idea how to show intimacy or who I was as a person.

Natalie looked at me, shaking her head. "Are you sure that you and I didn't have the same dad? I grew up with many of those same feelings, and I spent many hours in prayer asking God for wisdom and the ability to forgive."

"What did you come up with?" I asked intently.

"Even though I felt justified by my anger, I had passed judgment on my father. The moment I passed judgment on my father, I came under God's judgment. It says in the Bible,

> Do not judge, or you too will be judged. For in the same way you judge others, you will be judged, and with the measure you use, it will be measured to you.
> —MATTHEW 7:1

Forgiving my father was the very thing I needed to help me replace the void of intimacy and become whole enough to have a *healthy desire* for it rather than an *uncontrollable need* for it."

Natalie grabbed my hand and pulled me into the living room.

"Come here, I want to tell you a story that might help you. But you have to get comfortable. Lie down on the sofa and close your eyes. We are going to play a game that always helps me understand heavy concepts better. Jesus used parables to speak to His people so that they might understand His concepts that seemed so strange and contrary to the ways of the times. Let me attempt to paint a picture in your mind that might help expand your understanding."

Natalie sat on the floor close to me and began her story.

"For just a few minutes, let's use our imagination. Imagine there are two paths in front of you. One path is wide and inviting, meticulously paved and lined with an abundance of plush green trees. It also has a gentle, downward slope. In the distance you get a glimpse of a huge lake with many people participating in water sports. The sign reads 'Fun, Fun and More Fun.' You watch as many people walk past you, rushing toward the first bend in the road to see what other pleasures await them.

"However, the second path is a narrow one. It's covered with gravel, but you can see an abundance of fruit trees in the distance. This path has an unappealing upward grade. The sign over the path reads 'Love.' Very few people are choosing this path. You hesitate briefly as you ponder, *What is real love anyway?* So off you go down the wide path to join in the fun.

"As you round the first corner, the scenery begins to change. The trees are thinning out and clouds are rolling in. Just as you think you might turn around and head back, something wonderful appears. On one side of the path you see a circus. The sign over the entrance reads. 'Come and Play! All Rides and Food Free!' On the other side of the road is a wild party with a sign that reads, 'Unlimited Free Drinks.' In the distance you see a fabulous endless shopping mall. The entrance reads, 'Unlimited Credit.'

"You dedicate a day at each of these locations, and then you begin to get bored and move on. All of a sudden the road ends. You are greeted by unfriendly strangers with demanding faces.

"They shout, 'This is the end of the road. It's time to pay the toll.'

'What toll?' you ask.

"Immediately you are harnessed with a huge, heavy yoke. You are forced in line like a mule team and ordered to pull the burdensome load strapped behind you. You find yourself in the middle of a dry, sun-scorched dirt road. The temperature is 120 degrees. You glance around and wonder why so many others voluntarily accepted this task. But before your mind can wander further, you feel the sting of a whip on your back.

"'Forward!' booms a loud, deep voice from behind.

"You are pulling a coach, laden with stones, through the barren, dusty roads. The shouts become exceedingly confusing and ambivalent: 'Go this way! go that way!'

"You have no idea which direction he is telling you to go. You turn around to see which way he is pointing, which causes you to stumble and fall. Once again you feel the sting of the whip on your back again. Over and over, the direction changes.

"Days go by. Frustrated, hungry, and overburdened, you stumble on. Still your mind contemplates *Why?* and you continue to carry this load. Every time the whip hits your back you want to lift the yoke from your neck and run, but your legs become too weak to run. You fall flat on your face, and the many attempts to lift yourself are vain. Lying on the ground, you stare at the sky and reflect on days past when you served a much different master.

"After lying there for some time, you recall the path labeled, 'Love.'

"You are rudely snapped back to reality by the crack of the whip on your back. You think, *If I could just get to my knees and ask God's forgiveness, my life could be spared.* You struggle with one knee then the other. As your second knee hits the ground, you see Jesus standing in front of you. He reaches out and removes the harness from your neck. 'Come with Me, He says. 'Your debt has been paid.'

"Just that simply Jesus settles your account. He replaces your burdens with peace, joy, and eternal life. As you walk away to turn around and watch as Jesus takes the very burden you carried for months and puts it around His neck and takes your place, He turns to you and smiles, 'Go, and sin no more.' Your eyes fill with tears as you finally know what real love is.

"You stand there in awe. Your feet seem frozen to the ground. How can you walk away? Once again Jesus turns to you and says, 'Go. The Father has been waiting for you. He has prepare a special place for you.'

"Deborah, Jesus already paid the full price for your life with His. Remember that fear, anxiety, and guilt are not from God. Focus your mind on the life of Jesus and reclaim your rightful place in His kingdom. That's what redemption is all about. It means, 'to recover ownership of something by paying a specific sum, to set free or rescue.' Redemption is the deliverance upon payment of the ransom.

> God claimed you long ago. Now you need to claim Him as your Lord and Master. This is what the Lord says —he who created you, O Jacob he who formed you, O Israel! Fear not, for I have redeemed you; I have summoned you by name; you are mine.
>
> —ISAIAH 43:13

"You are redeemed! You've been bought with a price. You owed a debt you could not pay. Christ paid a debt He did not owe. He did it for you," Natalie said as she gently wiped the tears from my eyes.

"Are your stories always so descriptive?"

"They are now, Deborah. Only a short time ago, my situation was not too different from yours, and in the midst of it all, God dropped this gift into my spirit. And as I share it with others, He also gives me the right Scriptures to coincide with the situation."

"Well, it surely seems to have helped you!"

"It helped me know that if I'm going to accept God's forgiveness and love, than I too must forgive and love in the same manner.

"Deborah, you are probably not aware that I came from a broken home and a long line of alcoholism and abuse. Every time I thought I could climb out of that depression, my mind would say, *You'll never be anybody. You'll never amount to anything. Look **where** you've come from. Look **who** you've come from. Pull up a chair and get comfortable. You're not going anywhere.*

"For many years I placed my life's problems on my parents for what they had done to me. I used to wonder why I had the parents I had. But one day I heard these words in my head, 'You did not come *from* your parents; you came *through* your parents. You came from me. You are mine!'

"It didn't take me long to realize that it was the Holy Spirit telling me that I was claimed by God through grace, which is His unmerited favor. And I can tell you, that's better than any adoption papers you'll get here on earth."

I reached out and hugged Natalie and thanked her for sharing with me. She was just one of many who God used to so generously lift my burdens.

Understanding God's great love and forgiveness helped me to begin the process of lifting the blame from my parents and extending forgiveness. As I became able to look at my parents as people who had unresolved needs of their own, I was able to free them from their responsibility to meet my needs. "Parents who suffer from rejection generally communicate rejection to their children. In case after case when rejection is the problem, the person almost invariably says, 'My father could not show love.' Later, a person may conclude that his father did not love him. If a parent does not communicate love to a child, it creates a vacuum in his emotional being that leaves him empty inside, and emotionally crippled. This emptiness created by rejection gives the enemy a place to torment with self-rejection, a negative self-image, loneliness, depression, and an imaginary world."[8]

Rejection can be portrayed in many forms. My father didn't consciously reject me. He had not been taught how to love by his father. He carried his own void. Who knows how many generations our family was kept from the secret of love. The sad fact was that, evidently, no one knew how to break this generational curse.

I had to forgive my dad for the love I needed as a child that he unknowingly denied me. If Jesus died for his sins as well as for mine, I had to visualize my dad perfected in Jesus. How could I accept my forgiveness without extending the same forgiveness to my father. We both needed to be set free from past hurts to be free to know and love ourselves as Jesus loves us.

I looked at the circumstances surrounding my father's life. He was hurting too. No doubt he had material desires that were never fulfilled and as each child in our family was born, his dreams grew dimmer and dimmer. But I thank God He gave me a dad that chose life for his children over convenience, money and position.

Realizing my father did his best under the circumstances of his life released me from judging him. I was finally free to love my father for exactly who he was. Even though he was not the world's best father, he was the best he knew how to be at the time. He was the father God chose for me. God mercifully showed me I didn't come *from* my earthy father, but merely *through* him.

As I got a grasp on God's redeeming grace, I began to feel special. Did God really love *me* that much? It's one thing for Jesus to sacrifice His life for all mankind but quite another for Him to sacrifice His life for me. I'd been raised to think religion was a personal thing, but I hadn't considered the idea of a personal relationship with the big Man Himself.

I felt a new freedom as I joyously took two more steps forward. The words in the Bible began to speak to me personally. I began reading the Bible in the first person. It was as if God set a personal challenge before me. It was as if He handed me a cross with these simple instructions: "Go, and sin no more" (John 8:11).

Forgiving my father depicted but one battle in a war that took years to complete. I had to learn to see my dad with new eyes through forgiveness and then accept my inheritance from my heavenly Father in order to be a recipient of God's unconditional love. However, knowing what needed to be done seemed much easier than actually doing it.

But now, for the first time in my life, I had the taste of victory; the brick wall separating me from God was crumbling.

WHAT ABOUT MOM?

When God said there is none of you perfect, He did not exclude mothers. My mother controlled me without knowing it and loved me without showing it. Yet, even my mother was handpicked by God. I didn't have to understand it; I just had to believe it.

My mother and I were not close. When you're number four of nine children, *close* is a relative term. The term "crisis management" was invented by our family. With six brothers always into mischief and two adorable sisters that looked just like mom, I felt it was up to me to plan my life.

As I grew up it became clear the plans I had for my life and the plans Mom had were different. I'm sure Mom wanted the best for me, maybe even more than I wanted it for myself. She worked hard to see that her children grew up educated and experienced. But there were some experiences she had not counted on.

I will never forget the day I called my mother to tell her I was pregnant. I wanted to tell her in person but time and distance were not on my side. If there is one conversation a girl never forgets, it is the "Mom, I'm pregnant!" conversation, especially if she is unmarried.

My conversation went something like this. "Hello, Mom. How are you?"

"Fine. I haven't heard from you in a while."

"I know. I've been real busy and I've had a lot on my mind And..." And she interrupted by telling me everything my eight brothers and sister were doing, had done, and would ever do.

"Mom! Mom! I called you for a specific reason." She stopped abruptly. I felt my heart catch in my throat.

"What is it? Are you all right?"

"Well, I will be."

"What do you mean?" Hearing her frustration, I took a deep breath and blurted it out.

"I'm pregnant!"

"O Holy Mary, Mother of . . . ! What did you say?"

Did she really not hear what I said? Fresh panic set in as I thought I might have to say it over again. There was an interminable silence. Then Mother's voice came back with the sound of authority.

"Who is the father?" she demanded, knowing full well I hadn't dated anyone seriously in months.

Trying to avoid her "father" question I said, "Well, Mom, I'm still trying to deal with my pregnancy. I have not decided what I am going to do about the father." At this point, I was glad I was not standing face-to-face with her.

"Well who will provide for that child? *Someone* has to be financially responsible."

It seemed strange to me that "provision" was top priority at the moment. But then, I remembered that in a family of eleven, provision was always a priority.

"Don't worry about that," I said with resignation. "I will be responsible. It is *my* baby. God will help me find the way. . . ." My words trailed off as I thought about the Scriptures Carmen had given me the week before.

> So we say with confidence, "The Lord is my helper; I will not be afraid, What can man do to me?"
>
> —HEBREWS 13:6

> The Lord will guide you always; he will satisfy your needs in a sun-scorched land and will strengthen your frame.
>
> —ISAIAH 58:11

I knew better than to quote scripture to my mother. It was not my intention to pull rank on her maternal authority. I was thirty years old. How could I explain I didn't want her advice; I wanted her love and acceptance. Instead, our conversation ended rather abruptly when she replied, "Deborah, I don't know what to say."

"Just pray for me," I said.

"You know I will." There was a long silence like she really wanted to say more, but finally she just hung up the phone.

I could only imagine her disappointment. And I could already visualize her, after hanging up the phone, running to her bedroom, throwing herself upon the bed and crying, "Where did I go wrong?" This is how she always handled her problems.

I was well aware of the sacrifices she had made for the sake of my education, but I couldn't deal with my mother's problems right now. I didn't want to discount her feelings, but I had enough of my own feelings. I tried to put her reaction out of my mind. I realized that forgiving my mother would take time, so I left her emotions to the Lord and asked Him to give her peace. I had to break this news to many others and suffer through their reactions.

I had learned forgiveness is an act of love. God did not forgive me because I was worthy of forgiveness, but through the free gift of grace I was forgiven and thereby saved. I didn't even have to earn it. This grace is great stuff as well as contagious. I found healing and power in forgiveness, not only in being forgiven but in forgiving others, including myself and my mom. Through the act of forgiveness, I received the strength needed to face the world with my head held high.

Let us then approach the throne of grace with confidence, so that we may receive mercy and find grace to help us in our time of need.

—HEBREWS 4:16

BLESSINGS OR CURSES

Today's word for yesterday's sins is "dysfunctional." The world is full of dysfunctional people. Situations once labeled abnormal have become the norm. The typical family of today attend joint therapy classes. Hundreds of books are written about dysfunctional behavior. Support groups are available. Even the courts use the term dysfunctional to justify illegal behavior.

During the hippie movement of the sixties, the youth were a big target for the enemy. He found a very effective way of assuring the destruction of the future of this country through concentrating on man's selfish nature. New slogans were made famous on tee shirts, slogans like, "If it feels good do it," "What's in it for me?" or "It's my life!" They have replaced the Ten Commandments to "Whatever works best for me." Satan found a stronghold in their defiance and the disrespect for authority.

Today's youth find independence in the deceitful phrase "pro-choice." We are all pro-choice by our rebellious nature. We all like choices in whatever we do. But there are those who are deceived by the hidden choice that ultimately leads to life or death. That is a choice belonging exclusively to God. Yesterday's "free spirit" activist are today's "choice" supporters. The words may change, but the message stays the same: the shedding of responsibility and the emphasis on a four letter word, "self."

The sad part about past mistakes is the future results. Children are taught, or not taught, values, morals, consequences, responsibility and respect by their parents, their friends' parents and their grandparents, their teachers or mentors. But if parents were not taught these things, where do the kids learn how to uncover this lost treasure? How do we break this destructive cycle of selfishness and get back to the basics that made this country great, free and worth dying for?

After reading Marilyn Hickey's book, *Break The Generation Curse*, I clearly saw where God gives us a choice between curses and blessings. (See Deuteronomy 11:26–28, 27:15–26, 28:1–14.)

"God's Word also states that curses can be passed down from generation to generation."[9] "Things that harass and plague us like asthma, obesity, alcoholism, heart conditions are actually family or generation curses . . . problems which started way back with our ancestors and have been carried through right to today. What's worse, they won't stop here, but are passed on to our children and to our children's children!"[10]

Sins of sexual promiscuity and divorce are also curses that are passed on from generation to generation. This is a documented fact. If your parents were divorced, the odds are you will be divorced. I am a living example. My grandmother and grandfather on my mother's side were divorced, my mother and father are divorced, and I have also been divorced.

I can still recall the day my first husband announced our engagement to his very Catholic mother. At the time I was Catholic also. I expected her to be very happy for us. Instead she was polite, but less than enthusiastic. Later, she explained her concern to me. It was the fact that I came from a broken home and the odds of survival were not in our favor.

This was only one of the many obstacles that plagued my first marriage. Even though what she said was true, why didn't she tell me how to break the curse or get on her knees and intercede for us. I am sure it was not because she did not want to, but because she did not know how.

> My people are destroyed from lack of knowledge.
> —HOSEA 4:6

In the opening of the book, *Break The Generation Curse* a true story is told of two American families that left a lasting impression on me. It goes like this:

Max Jukes was an atheist who married a godless woman. Some 560 descendants were traced:

Three hundred ten died as paupers —150 became criminals—seven of them murderers —100 were known to be drunkards—and more than half of the women were prostitutes.

The descendants of Mac Jukes cost the United States government more than 1.25 million in 19th century dollars.

Jonathan Edwards was a contemporary of Max Jukes. He was a committed Christian who gave God first place in his life. He married a godly young lady, and some 1,394 descendants were traced:

Two hundred ninety-five graduated from college, of whom thirteen became college presidents and 65 became professors—three were elected as United States senators—three as state governors, and others were sent as ministers to foreign countries—30 were judges—100 were lawyers (one the dean of an outstanding law school)—56 practiced as physicians (one was the dean of a medical school)—75 became officers in the military—100 were well-known missionaries, preachers and prominent authors—another 80 held some form of public office, of whom three are mayors of large cities—one was the comptroller of the U.S. Treasury—and another was vice president of the United States. (See footnote pg. vii, Hickey.)

Not one of the descendants of the Edward's family was a liability to the government![11]

I know what it feels like to live under the curse. It's as though you have this big black cloud hanging over you. You can't amount to anything because of where you came from. Your heritage is a stench in your life with alcoholism, sexual promiscuity, physical and verbal abuse, and divorce is dinner-table conversation.

Without the gift of redemption, I never would have been able to accomplish enough in my lifetime to erase all the generational curses. As an adult, when things started going too good, I got scared. I lived in constant fear knowing it was only a matter of time before something went wrong. And it usually did. I was always running against the wind until I accepted Jesus Christ as Lord of my life. I cannot tell you what it means to me to be able to rise above past generations and claim a new heritage for my children and my children's children. I've been spiritually rich, and I've been spiritually poor, and I'm here to tell you, rich is best.

To help illustrate God's desire for you to make a personal choice about the direction of your life, I have composed the following passage:

Suppose God joined you for breakfast one morning. You are just sitting quietly pondering over life's newest trial, and He walks up and pulls up a chair and says, "Good Morning, _____! I have been wanting to talk to you. Do you have a minute or two?" Notice, God never forces Himself on you, He waits to be invited.

You know, _____, when I created you I had a purpose in mind for your life, and every part of your life is part of a plan to fulfill that purpose. I still remember making your eyes, your hair, your heart, your mind. There is no one else like you, and I love you very much.

"But I am a jealous God, and I am genuinely concerned about the path you have chosen for your life. You are missing out on all the blessings I reserved especially for you, as well as those I reserved for your children and your children's children. This saddens Me. I wish I could allow you to see into your future and know what a happy future I have planned for you. But that's against the rules.

"I am a patient God, and I will not pressure you into a commitment before you are really ready. But as I look at you and see you hurting, it breaks My heart. The time is right for you to make a choice. You can continue to stay in control and keep following the same path and all your sins, and the pain that goes with them will continue to reach you and your children unto the third and forth generations. Or, you can renew your life by beginning a relationship with Me. All that I ask is for you to love Me with all of your heart and keep My commandments. If you do this, I promise not only to lift your pain and suffering but also to lift it from your children's children, up to a thousand generations (Deut. 7:9). The choice is yours."

Then God slowly stands up and walks out the door, leaving you with a life-changing choice. You hold the choice of obedience. God even supplies the grace to overcome temptation.

"Of course, all of this must be done in complete faith in God's Word and in Jesus Christ. Believing Christ became a curse for us—as stated in Galatians 3:13–14—we now share in the blessings of Abraham if we choose to walk in obedience to God's Word."[12]

> See, I am setting before you today a blessing and a curse—the blessing if you obey the commands of the Lord your God that I am giving you today; the curse if you disobey.
> —Deuteronomy 11:26–28

> If you fully obey the Lord your God and carefully follow all his commands I give you today, the Lord your God will set you high above all the nations on earth. All these blessings will come upon you and accompany you if you obey the Lord your God.
> —Deuteronomy 28:1–2

CHAPTER 8

The Pains of Living in Two Worlds

I was entering my eighth month of pregnancy, and I no longer recognized the chunky little stranger in the mirror. My 5-foot-5 inch, 120-pound frame had totally rearranged despite my attempt at physical fitness. I once had an hourglass figure, but the sands had shifted. I tried to watch my weight by eating smart and exercising. Carmen and I established a walking routine of at least two miles, three to four times a week. Carmen stood guard over me everyday making sure I consumed all five food groups. When she wasn't busy feeding my body, she was feeding my spirit.

She would follow me from room to room, reading the Bible with heart and soul. Time and time again she would say, "Oh, listen to this part. Just one more chapter; this is really good." Carmen was an angel during my pregnancy. She always lifted me up when I was down. She was my loyal Lamaze coach even when the rest of the class were newlyweds. She was with me during my seven-month checkup. And when the doctor became alarmed at my sudden fluctuation in weight, he advised this could possibly mean twins. Too shocked to speak, I thought, *O God, no! Please no—not two!*

Since we learned this on a Friday, I would have the whole weekend to fret over this new event. What would I do with two or even worse, more than two? No matter how I looked at it or reasoned with it, more than one would be all consuming for me.

As we walked to the car, Carmen, trying to be comforting, said, "Debi, God never give us more than we can handle."

"Then this is the exception to the rule because I cannot handle two, or five, or however many more than one means," I snapped.

Why did everything have to get so complicated? The weight of this situation seemed heavier than ever before. I stayed in my room all day Saturday, feeling sorry for myself.

Early Sunday morning I decided I wasn't going to church. I think I was sort of mad at God. But Carmen kept insisting.

"OK, I'll go," I said. "But I'm only going for you. Don't expect me to participate in anything. I'm tired of praying. I'm tired of eating right. I'm tired of exercising. I'm tired of being pregnant, and I'm tired of being tired."

"Deborah, I wish I could tell you the plans God has for your life, but all I can do is point you to the Father. I've watched your faith grow and deepen with every passing day. I see you seeking the heart of God. If I can notice that, you can be assured that our heavenly Father has noticed. If you are feeling pushed to your limit right now, you can be sure it is the Father pushing you in a heavenly direction.

"We are told not to lean on our own understanding because we cannot understand the ways of God. Along with faith we must exercise our trust in Him. We are told to be confident that when God has begun a good work in you, He will carry it on to completion." (See Philippians 1:6.)

There was another long silence, and finally I asked quietly, "Don't you ever get tired of picking me up off the ground?"

"I ask God the same question about myself. He tells me that He will keep picking me up until I learn not to fall."

"Thank you, Carmen, for all that you are."

I wish I could say that everything Carmen told me made me ready to accept whatever came my way. But the best I can say is it did make sense. So I constantly worked on absorbing her godly wisdom into my spirit. But two babies! Two times the diapers! Two times the food! Two of everything!

After church Carmen invited a mutual friend over for lunch. I knew she was trying to keep me from thinking too much about my plight.

During lunch I decided to share the news about the possibility of twins with Marty, our guest. I no sooner got the words out of my mouth when I watched her face go into shock. She sat there speechless and starred at me.

"Are you kidding? Is this a joke?" she finally asked.

You see Marty wasn't the spiritual giant Carmen was. She saw my situation with different eyes.

"I wish it were a joke. I wish this whole experience were a joke and in the end I would have a good long laugh."

"I'm sorry. I didn't mean to be insensitive. What are you going to do?"

"I'll just have to sell one. That's all there is to it."
Carmen and Marty both stared at me to see if I was
kidding.

"Relax girls. I don't know what I'll do. But I refuse
to play the 'what if' game. I'm not going to think
about it until tomorrow."

"Oh, there goes Scarlet O'Hara again," remarked
Carmen, and we all laughed. But my laughter ended
quickly. I was standing by the kitchen sink rinsing my
dinner plate, and as I looked out the window I
couldn't believe what I saw. "Oh, no!" I said as I ran
from the room.

"What? What is it?" Carmen shouted as she followed me to my room.

"It's Bill! I saw his silver Mercedes pull up in front
of the house. Go look and tell me I'm wrong. Tell me
whoever is in that car is visiting the neighbor. Carmen
ran to the kitchen window. She came running back,
"It's him. It *is* him!" she shouted in a whisper. "It's Bill,
and he is getting out of the car." Marty stood in the
dining room, helpless. She was experiencing just a
small taste of my daily humiliation.

"How did he find me? What does he want? I
haven't seen him since before my pregnancy. Why is
he all of a sudden walking back into my life?"

"Just stay in your room. I'll tell him something,"
Carmen said with her mother tone.

I'd been so busy with my own problems I hadn't
taken the time to even think about Bill and why he
had stopped calling.

Carmen came back into the room and said, "He's
gone."

"What did he say?'

"He asked if you were here. When I told him you
were out—I didn't say out where; Anyway, he said to

tell you he'd been thinking about you and that he would call you tomorrow."

"But why?" I asked dazed. "Why now? If he really cared why had he waited until now?"

"Why don't you play the Scarlet game and think about that tomorrow?" Carmen quipped.

We all laughed and returned to the kitchen to the dishes.

"Deborah, you sure make my life appear boring," Marty observed.

"Do you want to trade?" I whipped.

"Not this year. I don't have the courage."

"Is that what it takes, courage? Someday I want to wake up with a purpose."

"Knowing you, that wouldn't be hard," Marty said as she gathered her things together. "I love you both. Dinner was great, and thanks for asking me. Please, if there's is anything I can do for you, let me know."

"Thanks, Marty; just keep in touch."

"Are you kidding? I'll stay tuned for sure. I have to hear how this all turns out."

It was late when Carmen and I finished the dishes, so I headed for my room. I was exhausted. But how was I going to sleep tonight with tomorrow's questions pounding my brain?

TOMORROW IS ANOTHER DAY

Daybreak came, and I couldn't decide if I should hurry or drag my feet. I wanted to know; yet, what if I really was carrying twins? I promised myself not to think about that possibility until . . .

I arrived a little early, but to no avail. The waiting room was full. I tried reading a magazine, but the best I could do was look at the pictures. After reviewing every magazine in the room, I began to pace. Finally my name was called.

In the doctor's office they prepped me and I don't know what else they did. All I wanted to hear was the bottom line. As I lay there waiting, the nurse painstakingly pointed to the picture on the screen. "There's a hand. See the hand? There's a head. Can you see the head? The baby is sitting up. That's good, and...."

I couldn't stand it any longer. "How many heads do you see?" I blurted out.

"Oh, there's just one!"

I wanted to jump up and kiss the nurse. But instead, I lay there thanking God and hearing very little after that.

The nurse said I could get dressed now. I went home happier than I had been in a long time.

I had totally forgotten about Bill when the phone rang. I thought it was Carmen calling to find out the results. I picked up the phone and said, "There's only one!"

"Deborah, is that you?"

I know I must have turned crimson red when I recognized Bill's voice on the other end of the phone.

"Oh, I'm sorry. I thought you were someone else."

"Obviously. There's only one what?"

"Nothing," I snapped. "Carmen said you stopped by yesterday. Why?"

"Well, I've been thinking about you, and I wanted to see how you're getting along."

"I'm fine, thank you. How are you?" I asked curtly.

"I know I haven't been much of a friend lately, but I can explain."

"A friend? Is that what you are? You walked out of my life the moment I really needed a friend. Seven months later you suddenly get concerned? There's a name for friends like that."

"Deborah, please let me explain."

"I'm listening."

"My wife was having me followed."

"Your wife?"

"Yes, you know that we've been negotiating a divorce settlement for the past two years. Well, we were in the final stages and she was trying to dig up some dirt on me so she could get a better settlement. I knew if she found out I was seeing you, she would drag you into this, and before long she'd be asking for a paternity test. I didn't want to bring you into my mess."

"You could have called?"

"I was afraid my phone lines were tapped. I didn't want to take any chances. I figured you had enough to deal with already."

"There's a phone at every gas station in town. Or did you think they were all bugged as well?"

"I just didn't know what to say. I guess my feelings were a little hurt too when I found out you were pregnant. I suppose I was jealous."

"I'm sorry, Bill. I'm not being fair."

"Don't apologize. You're right. I should have found a way to get through to you. But I'm happy to say that my divorce is finally official."

"I'm sorry. That must be hard."

"Not really. Two years ago it was hard to accept. A year ago it was slightly painful. Today I'm relieved to be moving forward again."

"How are your kids taking it?"

"Not good, but they're all adults now, and they'll have to learn to live with it just like I will."

"I'm sure time will help. I'm certainly counting on time to help me. I've had a lot of changes in my life, beside the obvious ones. I've found a new church, and

I've made a lot of great friends. I can honestly say my life is moving forward in a positive direction."

"That's great. When can I see you?"

"I don't know, Bill. I'm not so easy to look at anymore."

"I doubt that. I bet you look precious as an expectant mommy. Please let me come see you."

"Let me think about it for a little while."

"OK, that's fair enough. I'll call you next week."

"OK."

"It's great to hear your voice again, Deborah."

"Thanks. It's nice to have my friend back again."

Bill did call the next week. The following week he came for dinner. He wanted to know my plans and if I needed anything. I assured him I had things under control and didn't need anything. Seeing him brought back a lot of old memories. He represented a lifestyle I'd left behind, and I knew I would never be that person again. How did I explain it to Bill?

I asked Bill not to call me for the next few months. I told him I needed time to get back on my feet without leaning on anyone but God. He said he understood but if I needed anything, to call.

MY NEXT SURPRISE VISITOR

Six weeks later on a Friday at 2:45 P.M., I called Carmen at work and said,

"It's time!

She said, "Are you sure?"

"Yes! I'm sure!"

"I'll be right home."

Then I called Mom, so she could inform the family and catch the next flight. It was about 3:30 P.M. when Carmen pulled into the driveway. She came running into the house out of breath and said, "Come on!"

"Not yet! I need to take a shower and wash my hair. Who knows when I'll be able to wash my hair again."

"Deborah! We have to go!"

"No. My water has broke, but I haven't started contractions yet. Why don't you call the doctor and see if I need to go to the hospital now or if I should wait for the contractions to begin. In the meantime, I'll take a quick shower."

Minutes later Carmen came into the bathroom yelling. "We need to go to the hospital now. I told them your water broke, and they don't want infection to set in."

"OK. I'll be ready in about twenty minutes."

About 4:30 P.M. we hit the road just in time for rush hour traffic. That's when I felt my first contraction. *So that's what they were talking about*, I thought to myself. I didn't dare tell Carmen my contractions had started. She was nervous enough.

In the delivery room they told me the baby hadn't turned around but was still sitting upright. I required a C-section. By 5:59 P.M. they were lifting the baby out. I can still remember hearing those words.

"It's a . . . It's a . . ."

"It's a what?" I yelled.

"It's a girl!"

My head fell back into my pillow, relieved that my daughter had finally arrived. The nurse brought her to me and laid all of my baby's seven pounds, five ounces on my chest. She was perfect and beautiful. Her name would be Felicia Nicole, meaning "Joyful Conquer." I had labored for months over baby name books trying to find the perfect name. I wanted it to have significance. I remembered how much it meant to me when my mother told me I was named after Deborah in the

Bible. As I grew older, the more significant it became.

I was still in recovery when my mother arrived from St. Louis. I can still see the smile on her face as she grabbed my hand and said, "Deborah, I'm so proud of you."

"Isn't she beautiful?"

"Yes, she's beautiful," she said, tears filling her eyes. "You didn't give me much time to get here; plus, you are two weeks early."

"Felicia must have my impatience. Once I decide to do something why wait?"

"Your father will arrive this evening, and he will come to see you tomorrow."

"Are you OK with that, Mom?" I asked, knowing that my parents had chosen not to be in the same room with each other for over ten years since their divorce. We were careful to arrange for my mom to stay with Carmen and my dad to stay with my brother.

"Don't worry about me. I'll be fine. If he doesn't behave, I'll just borrow your bedpan."

We both laughed, and before I drifted off to sleep I asked, "Mom, would you please check on Felicia and hold her until I get my strength?"

"I'd love to, Sweetie. You just get your rest."

I knew that between Carmen and Mom, Felicia would have to want for nothing but rest.

I didn't see much of Felicia for the first twenty-four hours. We were both pretty drugged up and exhausted. But soon after that, I couldn't get enough of her. When the nurse would come to take her back to the nursery, I would hide her under the cover. The nurse would just smile and say, "I'll be back in a little while. You know you need to get your rest too in order to heal."

In the five days we were in the hospital I watched

Felicia melt the hearts of my mother and father as they stayed in my room together. I watched them rock her as they held her tightly. I caught them glancing at each other in a knowing way as they remembered the many newborns they had shared together. My parents even began to go out to lunch and dinner together without a referee. Felicia was like a magic potion. The meaning of her name was already unfolding.

A week after Felicia's birth, my parents brought us home.

Carmen mailed out the birth announcements, and by now, everyone knew about Felicia's birth, including Jim.

I wonder how it feels to have the U.S. mail bring you news that you are a father. I admit I was a little disappointed about not hearing from Jim. Strangely, I received flowers in the hospital from Bill. I had no idea how he even knew I was in the hospital, especially since I went in two weeks early. Even though Jim hadn't called me up to this point, I thought at least he would call when he received the birth announcement. I couldn't stand it, so I called him to tell him he had a beautiful daughter. He was very polite. He said, "I am sure, if she looks anything like you, she's beautiful."

Then he said, "Thanks for calling."

A few days later, I was still haunted by the nothing-ness of our phone conversation. How could anyone know there is a newborn child that is flesh of their flesh and not be at all curious about what she looks like. My feelings went back and forth from pity to rage. Nothing could change the fact that Jim was her biological father. In order to clear my head and satisfy my sense of obligation, I sat down and wrote him this letter:

Dear Jim,

I have so many things I would like to say, and I am not sure how and where to begin. So I have asked God's wisdom in dealing with our communications. When I called you the other day to let you know about our daughter, I did it with love and forgiveness. However, I felt your coldness and even your sense of denial. This really hurt me. It was not easy for me to make that call, and I did not do it for myself but for our daughter.

Rejection is one of life's hardest blows to handle and I would like to protect our daughter from that if at all possible. Someday the truth will be revealed to her and she will ask me why. The questions she will ask will not be easy to answer, and it will break my heart to tell her that her father never wanted to see her or did not care if she was even alive.

Jim, I know I told you I wanted nothing from you, but there is one thing I would like to ask of you. I am only sorry that I have to ask it of you instead of your volunteering it. I would like you to meet your daughter, to see her face, to get to know her if possible. I will not do anything to jeopardize your career or your public image. I have nothing to gain from that. I want our daughter to be proud of her father.

I did not ask to become impregnated by you and carry this child for nine months without the support of a loving husband, but nothing can change the fact that we are the parents of this child. I would not do anything to change the fact I am now a mother. She is a blessing in my life, and I love her dearly.

If you think I want money, I've already told you I expect nothing. I am aware that I make more money than you do as a public servant. I also know that I will have some rough times ahead, but I am trusting God to provide the financial support we need. I have an extraordinary and supportive roommate and many great friends. The singles group at church has adopted me and our daughter. Our daughter has about 100 godparents. The Lord has blessed me not only with a lovely daughter but also with the means to take care of her.

The only thing I cannot provide for her, no matter what I do, is the acceptance she will need from her father. I feel like there is a side of her that I will never know. I was hoping she would look more like me. My mother says she looks more like you. But I think it is too early to tell.

I have decided to tell our daughter the truth from the beginning. I think this will be better than throwing it at her later in life. Somehow I will explain who her father is and that he lives very far away. I have a picture of you that I am saving for her.

Jim, I am not saying I know all the right answers or the best way to handle this crazy situation, but I am trying. I want the best for our daughter. If you have any suggestion, I would be glad to listen.

Sincerely,
Deborah

Jim never called me again, which is something I will never understand. But He would have to live with his decision. And I would live with the decisions I made for me and my baby. I couldn't afford to let pride enter into any of my decisions. I knew someday my child would come to me and want to know the whys of it all. So I carefully journalized my feelings and kept copies of the letters I sent to Jim.

BABIES TAKE BUCKS

I was thirty years old and earning over $32,000 dollars a year when I discovered I was pregnant. I had just been promoted twice in quick succession and was on the fast track to worldly success. I had planned to work until six weeks before the scheduled birth. Due to complications with my pregnancy, I was forced to quit two weeks earlier than planned.

I had been with the company for thirteen years and had accumulated seventy hours of sick pay and eight weeks of maternity leave for which I would be paid. This meant I could receive pay for three months without returning to work. My excellent insurance plan helped me with many, but not all, of my medical expenses.

I thanked God every day for a comfortable three-bedroom house and a roommate who had a gentle, giving spirit. The Lord had blessed my life with the provisions I needed. But even with all this working in my favor, I still struggled financially because of my commitment to stay home with my baby until she was six months old. When I weighed the choice of material security versus her emotional security, there was no choice. Since I would be a single parent, I wanted to form a bond that no one could break.

Months before Felicia's birth I had tried to pay off my debts and save enough money to get us through my leave of absence. Still, it was not enough. When my daughter was only four months old, I had depleted our funds, and I still owed three doctors a total of $1,500! The excessive expense was because of the unexpected C-section. And now, I had reached the maximum allowance on my credit cards. Nonetheless, I believed the Lord would provide.

Nothing seemed forthcoming and, as I have mentioned before, patience is not a virtue of mine. I lost patience with God and sought help at the last place I thought I would ever go—the state aid agency.

At the agency, I was passed from office to office, and kept running into the same dead end. They kept asking me if I knew the father. "Yes," I answered, "but due to personal reasons, I am not at liberty to disclose his name."

They informed me that if the state were to help me financially, it would need to know the father's name so they could attempt to recover their expenses. I understood their position. It was fair, but I felt in my heart that nothing good would come from disclosing the father's name. It would ruin his reputation and possibly end his political career.

The agency offered me one alternative. If I sold my two-year-old car and bought a car costing less than $300, and if I would say I did not know who the father was, then they had three different programs for which I would qualify. The options they gave me left me with no choice. I would lose so much more than they could ever provide if I were to agree to these demands. I decided right then and there to trust the Lord, regardless.

I left the state agency feeling very discouraged, but assured in my heart that I was doing the right thing.

The very next day I received monetary gifts through our church office from the members and Christian friends who had heard about my situation and wanted to help. Believe me, it was a substantial gift, enough to pay my remaining hospital bill and cover my expenses so that I would be able to stay with my baby until she was six months old. I was overwhelmed with gratitude and joy at God's faithfulness.

The next two months of my life were so blessed! Friends came to hold and admire my baby daughter. Several of the women shared confidences with me which they had locked up inside themselves for years. I found myself being the comforter instead of the one comforted. God graciously provided a ministry for me during that time to lift and encourage others, which still exists today. God is so good!

THE LAST TEMPTATION

It was now only a month before I had to return to work. I didn't like to think about it, but I had to recognize that it was a fact. So I began my search for appropriate child care. I visited place after place after place. The more I searched, the more discouraged I became. Every child care place was filled with wall-to-wall cribs, crying babies, and frustrated help. I could not help myself as tears swelled in my eyes. Where did the American family go? What kind of future does a child have when raised by strangers? Would my daughter now become just another statistic housed in the baby homes of America?

Growing more discouraged by the day, I prayed. "O God, don't leave me now. I need Your strength more than ever. I am running out of options. What am I supposed to do?"

I prayed and thought and prayed some more. Then I remembered something I had read the day before.

> You will weep no more. How gracious he will be when you cry for help! As soon as he hears you, he will answer you.
> —ISAIAH 30:19

Drying my eyes, I sincerely thought about what I wanted for my child so I would know how to pray.

I wanted my little girl to have personal care by someone special. I wanted a Christian home that would nurture my little girl like I would. So I placed an advertisement on the church bulletin board.

> I am looking for a wonderful loving, Christian, patient person to care for a precious six-month-old girl. She needs a warm and loving place to stay for a few hours a day, Monday through Friday. Please call.

Within a week an angel appeared in the form of a wonderful baby-sitter. She was a friend of a friend with two older children, and a stay-at-home mom with lots of experience. She lived close to me, so it was very convenient. Another blessing from God! Why did I ever doubt?

> Delight yourself in the Lord and he will give you the desires of your heart.
> —PSALM 37:4

Prior to returning to work, I had already applied for a transfer to another department. I could not keep my current high pressure, traveling job with a baby. Two weeks later I was transferred to a position in the airport terminal. The position required no travel and provided a late shift from 4 P.M. to midnight. Thanks be to God, I could stay home with the baby during the day!

Carmen worked a day shift, and took care of little Felicia during the evenings. There were many nights I sat at work wishing I could be the one rocking Felicia to sleep; nevertheless, I knew she was in good hands. It was more important to be home in the morning when she woke up ready to be cuddled and to play.

Every night after work I would sneak into her room to touch her soft skin and experience the aroma of the sweet baby smells lingering in her room. I stood there marveling at God's miracle. It soon became hard to imagine my life without her. Before I left her room each night I prayed this prayer over her.

Dear Lord,
   I pray that You watch over this sweet little life as she sleeps.
   Have her to dream of heavenly places and beautiful faces.
   O merciful and loving Father, bridge the gap between the love I can give Felicia as a single parent and the love she needs to grow in the fullness of Your grace and joy.

Then I would go quietly from her room, knowing it would not be long before she would call for me in her very persistent baby way.

Felicia was an early riser. I liked to believe it was because she could not wait to see her mommy's face every morning. Whatever the reason, it was that thought that gave me the strength to live on five hours sleep—on a good night.

Fortunately, my new position had very little stress and required no creative thinking, while my benefits and pay remained the same. Yet another gift from God!

I worked at the airport in the airline's private membership club for frequent travelers. It was a large, quiet, posh facility away from the noise and hassle of the rest of the airport. For an annual fee, members reserved private meeting rooms where they could make telephone calls, use the computer, watch television, catch up with paper work, or just sit in the private lounge and socialize over their drinks.

My job was one of a glorified receptionist and secretary. We were there to take the hassle out of traveling for those who traveled for a living. Sounds great, huh?

I had only one problem with this job. Serving men! You know, those creatures God created first, and when He realized where he went wrong He thought He'd try again and created woman. If there was one message that was written all over my face at this time in my life it was, "All Men Beware!" I had to trust God every day in this job. The good points far outweighed the bad. I could sacrifice dealing with men as long as they stayed in their place, far away from me, or at least on the other side of my very large and very wide desk.

You may laugh, but I was used up. My heart that once looked like Swiss cheese had now been turned to cottage cheese, and God was the only solid thing holding it together. The men I was attracted to were not good for me. In other words, I was a poor judge of character. So I told God it was OK with me if I remained single forever. However, if this was not His plan for my life, *He* would have to choose my lifetime mate.

"But Lord, beware! I am not going to make it easy for You. I must be reassured by miraculous measures a mate is your choice for my life."

Not long after I returned to work, Bill breezed into the club with a female companion. He didn't notice me at first. But when his eyes caught mine, he quickly escorted his friend out of site. In a matter of minutes He was back, standing in front of me, wearing his charming smile.

"It's great to see you again."

"Thank you. It's nice to be back to work."

"When can we get together?"

"It looks like you're tied up right now," I quipped.

Ignoring my comment, he said, "I'll be back in a few days. How about dinner next week?"

"I don't know, Bill. I've been out of the swing of things for a long time, and I'm not so sure I'm ready right now."

"Please! We really need to talk."

"About what?"

"I'm not giving up until you say you'll at least meet me for a drink."

"I'll think about it."

"Great! I'll call you when I get back." He started to walk away and then stopped. He turned back toward me, leaning over the counter and said, "You look fantastic! I sure missed you!" he smiled and made his exit.

Why was I so disturbed? After all, I am the one who told him I needed time and space. So why did this encounter bother me so much? Could I be jealous? Surely not. We'd *always* maintained a platonic relationship. At least that's the way I characterized it.

I refused to waste any more time thinking about it. Now that my life held a whole new purpose, I was determined to guard my time concerning outside activities. My heart and my first priority was at home. I decided to maintain my "All Men Beware!" motto.

When Bill returned, he called just as he'd promised. I decided I may as well meet him and get this over once and for all. We met at a safe, public place where I wouldn't be so nervous. Bill wasted no time in telling me what was on his mind.

"I want to take care of you and your child."

"My child's name is Felicia."

"Well, I haven't had the pleasure of meeting her. But I'd like to," he said as he grabbed my hand. "Come, go with me for little bit," he said as he pulled me up and headed for the door.

"Where are we going?"

"I promise I'll have you back in an hour."

We drove to an exclusive area in Las Colinas. He parked his car on a hill, which appeared to be the highest point in the area. Bill said, "Let's take a walk."

"Where? There's nothing but vacant land?"

"You'll see. And as we walked, he pointed to the area. "See this land on the hill?"

"Yes."

"I'm buying it. I want to build *our* house on it."

I was speechless. I thought I was used to Bill's unusual surprises, but I'd been away from the fast life for a long time. So I just listened as Bill went on to paint his picture of the way he thought things should be.

"You and your daughter will want for nothing."

I was still speechless, and I stood there in silence thinking about Felicia. Part of me wanted to reach out and grab this dream before it got away. The other part of me laughed at the irony of this situation as I thought about the temptation of Jesus. In Luke's Gospel, he tells how Jesus had fasted for forty days and nights and was hungry when the devil offered Him food and the kingdom. The devil then took Jesus to the highest point of the temple of Jerusalem and asked Him to prove Himself.

Was this my test? Was God asking me to choose between what man could offer and what He could offer? Whom could I trust? Who had stood by me and comforted me?

I wish I could say the answer was easy, but it wasn't. In the natural, it would have been the answer to all my financial worries. But God's grace sustained me. Though I was tempted, I did not yield. I broke off my relationship with Bill. And God showed me His faithfulness once more as He blessed my life over and over. To this day I have never looked back on my decision.

CHAPTER 9

After the Storm God Promises a Rainbow

I'm afraid I've forgotten my membership card," he grinned, as he strode confidently into the Admirals Club. He was tall, jaunty, and seemingly a very well-possessed young man.

"What is your last name, Sir?" I asked in my best business voice.

"Oh, you don't need to bother yourself with looking it up. I'm honest."

"Trying to ignore his beguiling demeanor, I said, again in a very professional voice, "It will just take a minute to verify your membership."

Looking very innocent, he repeated, "Oh, come on. I'm an honest guy!"

I laughed and said, "May I have your last name? Let's just call it job security," I snickered.

"What's so funny?" he asked.

"A man who says he is honest!" I replied as I continued my search for his name. "And where do all the honest men in the world live?" I asked as his file came up.

"In Tulsa."

"Tulsa, Oklahoma?" I questioned, looking at his file.

"Yes," he answered hesitantly.

"And what do honest men in Tulsa do besides work?"

"My hobby is running," he answered with a smile.

"If I lived in Tulsa, I would run too. I would run right out of that city *and* that state for that matter."

He just laughed at me, but instead of walking away, as he was supposed to, he continued to stand in front of my desk.

"Have you ever *been* to Tulsa?"

"Yes, twice. Both times were unpleasant experiences."

"Maybe it was the company you kept."

"Possibly," I smiled thinking surely he would go now. His friendly curiosity was making me a little uncomfortable.

My co-workers giggled with amusement at my expense. It was obvious they could see my frustration, but enjoyed watching me squirm. I was not good at small talk, nor did I want to practice now. However, he was very easy to look at, apparently single, and he had these cute little dimples when he smiled. He had all the markings of a man who could threaten my, "All Men Beware" motto. What happened to my knack for dumping a dude? Unbelievably, my mouth was all thumbs. This whole situation was giving me sweaty palms, always a telltale sign I was getting nervous. But, thank God, time was on my side. Eventually, he would have to catch a plane and I could regain my composure. Finally, he went to make some telephone calls. But before he left, he said, "I am going to write you a letter on honesty."

My quick comeback was, "Oh, this ought to be good. By all means take your best shot. And please send it to this address," I quipped, flipping him my card. *This ought to be entertaining if nothing else.* I thought.

Several days later as I was checking my mail, I couldn't believe my eyes. Here was a letter from Tulsa, Oklahoma! Surprise, surprise! It was from a George Robertson, the man who was to write the infamous letter on honesty. I tore the letter open and began to read. His letter consisted of several instances of how he used honesty in dealing with his friends and business relationships

At the end of his letter, Mr. Robertson included a few comical survey questions to test the waters for further communication. It had been along time since I had a good laugh, and the stories were humorous. This gave me a great inspiration. Here was a man who said he was always honest, even when it hurt. I decided to respond to his letter and put him to the test.

For a week I proceeded to write down all the questions I wanted a man to answer honestly. I wrote down questions about issues in many different areas, question that are important to know right up front in a relationship. With thirteen years of dating experience, this survey was easy to pull together. I also asked friends and co-workers if they had any contributions to make. I had the attention of a professed honest man, and I was not about to pass up a opportunity to milk his honesty for all it was worth.

I compiled a twelve page survey. The survey was titled, "Concerned Women of America." It began with three qualifying questions. Do you smoke? Have you ever smoked? Will you ever smoke? If the answer to any of these questions is yes, you have completed this survey. Please mail it to the enclosed address. If the answer to all the above questions is no, then please continue.

I was allergic to cigarette smoke, and to me, smoking represented a lack of discipline that brought with it a trail of unpleasantness. If someone was unable to care about their own well-being, then I was certain they could not be concerned enough for mine. Did I mention that tolerance was not one of God's gifts to me, at least not in this area and not at this time in my life.

The survey also consisted of a diverse range of topics divided into four basic areas, the first of which were "spiritual" questions. I started with easy questions like, "Who made you?" and worked into much deeper questions like, "From where do you draw your strength, wisdom, and understanding?" I was not about to divert my life from it's spiritual direction—not now or ever. Jesus Christ was the wind in my sail, and though my course might change, my direction would always be with the Wind.

The second section of the survey dealt with "psychological" questions. Do you love your mother? Do you love your father? Have you always loved your mother? Have you always loved your father?

Too many times I became involved with men who had unsolved psychological problems that led back to unhealed relationships with their mother, and eventually I became their voodoo doll. I once dated a guy who found it easier to wallow in self-pity about his unpleasant childhood than accept responsibility for his life and move beyond his misfortunes. For seven years he paid a psychiatrist to listen to his tales of woe. I thought it pretty sad to pay a hundred dollars an hour to receive sympathy instead of healing, especially for seven years. How much sympathy does it take to motivate someone to take responsibility? Let's see, fifty-two weeks at $100 a day for seven years, comes to $36,400. That's a lot of sympathy. I thought about offering to listen for half that price, but after a little thought I decided my time wasn't worth that at any price.

Before entering the third section of the survey I wrote the word, INTERMISSION. I figured by now he might need a break from all his honesty. Then I continued my infamous survey with "self-disclosure." This section included questions like, What do you like most about yourself? What do you like least about yourself? Would you label yourself a giver or a taker?

The last area covered many miscellaneous questions. Some questions were just for fun and others were full of pertinent information like, Do you like children? How do you see yourself as a father? And finally, describe your idea of the ultimate evening out with a desirable date.

I then sent the survey to Tulsa for processing. I had no idea if he would answer the survey. At this point I was only curious. Even if I never heard from him again, I had fun composing it. The survey allowed me to consider what was important to me and the priorities they held in my life. Without realizing it I defined what I wanted in a mate.

To my surprise, a week later I received the survey back in the mail with a note that said it took him three-and-a-half hours to complete. Also, when I got home from work that night, there was a message on my telephone answering machine. It said, "Hello! This is the mayor of Tulsa. We heard from a reliable source you have been bad-mouthing our community. Maybe it is time for you to visit and see the true heart of our city. You will be contacted soon by one of our very reputable and very honest citizens to arrange the details of your anticipated visit."

Humor! This was good. It reminded me of one of my father's favorite characteristics. That night I sat down and read the fully completed survey. His honesty amazed me. The significant aspect of George's answers to the survey questions were in the fact that his answers were not tailored to my expectations or needs. At this time he had no idea of either. At this point I could only assume his answers were exactly how he felt. He came across as honest, intelligent, and introspective. Although his answers on his current spiritual life were not as solid as I would have liked, they showed promise. He stated he grew up in the Assemblies of God Church, so I knew he had a good background. Now I needed to find out which direction he was moving in spiritually. On this issue there would be no compromising. He called a few days later to see if he passed the test.

"I thought about coming to Dallas to see you this weekend. I need to come see my folks, do you think we might get together on Saturday?"

"I'm afraid I'll be tied up with my daughter's first birthday celebration. Maybe another time." I said politely. "Besides, I'm not sure I'm ready to see you again," I added, which really opened the door.

"Why?" he asked.

"I get sweaty palms just talking to you on the phone."

"Do I make you that nervous? I'm really quite harmless."

"Said the spider to the fly," I replied.

"You can always bring a friend if you're too uncomfortable to go out with me alone."

"Considering your height, maybe I'll bring several friends."

"You will be perfectly safe because, remember ..."

"I know, I know, your an honest man." We both laughed.

"Haven't I convinced you yet?"

"I hear what you say and I read what you wrote, but I'm from the 'Show Me' State of Missouri."

"OK, when?"

"When what?"

"When can I show you?"

"Soon!" I said, and invited him to call again. I just needed time.

A few days later I received a card from Tulsa. I opened it to find a birthday card for Felicia and a coupon for deodorant. George wrote, "In case you're wondering, the deodorant is for your sweaty palms."

I loved his humor.

After many long and in-depth telephone calls, George flew to Dallas for our first official date. I made sure that all our activities were surrounded by many friends. On Friday night, we attended a going-away party for a friend, a wedding on Saturday afternoon and dinner with his friends on Saturday night.

On Sunday, George needed to spend some time with his parents. But for a day and a half we had enjoyed each other's company while in the company of others. I watched George cautiously from a distance; he appeared very self-assured and comfortable with whatever situation presented itself. He didn't seem to work at impressing me. He was gracious not only to me but also to all my friends. Even Carmen, my roommate, who was suspicious of anyone who showed me attention, seemed to like him.

TRUTH *AND* CONSEQUENCES

It was Saturday, 11 P.M. We sat in my driveway reflecting on the past thirty-six hours. He sat comfortably in the diver's seat, turned toward me, and I sat hugging the door, eyes front.

My thoughts flashed back to years of dating. These were the moments I hated most. At the end of every date as we pulled into the driveway, I wanted to jump out of the car and run into the house, waving good-bye as the front door graciously closed behind me. That was *my* idea of the perfect way to end any first date.

George, however, had a much more mature way of handling the situation. He was simply honest and up front.

"Well, where do we go from here?" He asked.

Stunned at his candor, my hand dropped from the door handle as I turned to look at him.

"The way I see it," he said, "we have two options. The first option is to just be friends, and whenever I am in town I can call you and see if you're available to go out. The second option is to move toward the possibility of a long-term relationship and work out how we can best accomplish that relationship long distance."

George had surprised me with his candor, and then I surprised myself as I said the first thing that came to my head.

"I have enough friends," I responded without much thought. *Oh great Deb, now look what you've done. You have now given this man only one option. Why oh why don't I think before I speak.* Now embarrassed, I wished I could take back the words I'd said so quickly and so carelessly. It was as if those words came out of someone else's mouth. Now I felt vulnerable and uncomfortable. I didn't want him to think I was desperate or easy, but what else could he be thinking? Well, now that I'm in this deep I might as well just take the plunge.

"I just want you to know that the next man I sleep with will be my husband."

There was dead silence for what seemed like hundred years. *Well, that should do. That should send him packing*, I thought.

Breaking the silence, George said, "Don't you think it's a little premature to talk about this?"

"No! I've paid the consequences of shallow relationships in the past, and I am not going back there. I don't want to wait till we have feelings for each other and get our feelings mixed up with our brains. Then we're unable to make clear and reasonable choices. I have to let you know right up front, how important this is to me so you can let me know if you can honor my request. On this issue there can be no compromise!" I must have sounded like a freight train rattling on and on before he could get a word in.

Finally when I stopped, he calmly and politely said, "Why don't we take some time to think about what we both want out of this relationship."

Think about it? Now there was a strange concept, obviously his idea. So while I was thinking about what George had said, he asked me if I wanted him to walk me to the door. "*Thank you, Jesus!*" I whispered to myself.

"Thank you, but I will be just fine. It was a lovely evening," I replied as I stepped out of the car and walked to the door. I turned and waved as he drove off, then quickly dashed into the haven of my home.

Giggling and shaking my head, I reflected back on our conversation. I probably made a fool of myself, but I was at peace with what I said. I thought God was probably gently laughing at me, but I also knew He was puffed up with pride. Whether or not George ever called me again was of little importance to me. That night I felt God restored my self-esteem and confidence so I could be a fool for Jesus, if necessary, and rejoice in it.

George continued to call. We enjoyed many long telephone conversations, sharing everything from the simple details of the day to our deep inner convictions. There was safety knowing he was several hundred miles away. The distance gave me the freedom to drop my defense long enough to get to know him. I felt the Lord softening my heart.

One day I told George I was going to Philadelphia for the weekend.

"Why?" was all he said.

"I feel like I need to resolve some issues with Jim." George knew about Jim, for I had laid all this out to him in my many conversations.

"What issues are there to resolve?" he asked, puzzled.

"I just can't understand how someone can know they have a child and not want to see their face. I want Jim to see his daughter."

"But why put yourself through the possibility of yet another rejection. Hasn't he already made his position clear? Why are you moving backward instead of forward?"

"I hurt for my daughter. How will it affect her when she's old enough to comprehend the circumstances behind her conception? What do I tell her when she realizes the man who helped make her did not care enough to even be curious about what she looked like? Do I say, 'Sorry, honey but your father considered you an inconvenience.'"

The tears began to flow, and I found myself apologizing for dragging George into my problems.

"I wish I could help, but I don't think forcing the issue will make things any better. Why don't you think about it for a while."

"But I have already called Jim and told him I was coming."

"You did? What did he say?"

"What could he say? He knows he can't refuse to see me. He's a public figure."

"Deborah, I wish you'd just think about this. Promise me you will think about it, and I'll call you in a few days."

Well, I thought about it alright. I could think of nothing else. I thought about praying and asking the Lord to show me what to do. And it was as though He said to me, *Why ask guidance when you know, deep down, what you should do.* I tossed and turned all night. Why was I trying to improve on past mistakes?

The next day I called Jim back to tell him I wasn't coming. All he said was "OK."

What a waste of time that would have been! I guess that's why God put our eyes in the front of our heads instead of the back. That way we can only see where we are going and not where we've been.

OLE FAITHFUL

Only a few months after George and I began to date, my doctor discovered a rather large tumor growing behind my ear. This was sudden and devastating news to me. He advised me that I needed surgery as soon as possible and scheduled me to see a specialist immediately. I felt uncomfortable about the urgency of the doctor's request, and I was afraid to ask him what he thought. I decided to save my questions for the specialist. I dreaded going to the specialist alone but I didn't want to discuss my problem with anyone else either. I didn't want to hear any "war stories" about what happened to them nor did I want to hear about any dearly departed relatives.

However, when George came in that weekend, he suspected something and asked, "Is there anything wrong? You don't seem to be your usual cheery self." So I told him point blank what the doctor said. He was so sweet, but said very little.

Monday morning came, and I drove downtown to the specialist's office. It was located in one of the local hospitals. To me, hospital halls seem so sterile, long and echo. I felt scared and alone. As I walked into the waiting room, there was George, sitting there reading a newspaper. I couldn't believe my eyes!

"What are you doing here?

"I didn't want you to be alone today."

"But how did you get here?"

"I drove."

"When?"

"I left home this morning about four. I was afraid I might not make it if I flew."

"I can't believe it," I said, hugging him tightly.

"I can't stay long, but I'll be here until the doctor gives you the diagnosis."

The specialist advised me he could not tell if the tumor was malignant without a performing a biopsy. My doctor, who was attending the specialist, told me I might want to "put my affairs in order—just in case."

Just in case? I screamed inwardly! Then, more calmly, I asked myself, *Just in case of what? Did I dare ask or did I already too clearly know just what he was saying?* The surgery was scheduled in three days.

Once again I found myself saying, "Why, God?" Why would You give me a child only to have her end up an orphan?" I'd spent my life falling down and trying to pick myself up again, but this was a pretty hard fall, maybe even fatal!

I just had to trust God. Where else could I go? Who else had the power to heal? He was doing a good job at healing my mind, so why not trust Him with my body.

I quickly put together a will for the custody of my daughter and then I sat down and wrote her a long letter. Tears involuntarily rolled down my cheeks as I thought of the possibility that she would not remember her mother.

My prayer that night went like this:

> "O, God! Can You hear me? You have shown me Your compassion and love as You have restored my battered heart. Surely it was not to break it once again. Teach me to put my full trust in You alone. Help me to accept Your will for my life."

The day of my surgery was a strange day. My father and George came with me to the hospital. I saw fear in their eyes, And I, too was fearful, but I knew Carmen and my church were praying for me.

I looked with new appreciation upon everything I saw that day, thinking, *This may be the last time I will be able to see the things that I take for granted everyday.* The sun looked brighter, the trees looked greener, and the sky looked bluer than ever before.

Both my father and George were very quiet that morning. I didn't feel much like talking either.

At the hospital, I was prepped for surgery. The last

thing I remembered was studying the faces of those I loved as they wheeled me to surgery.

The next thing I remembered was struggling to open my eyes. And as I did, George, leaning over me, gently whispering in my ear, "Your going to be OK, Deborah. The tumor is benign." Praising my faithful God, I drifted back into a peaceful sleep.

I never forgot George's constant support that day. In all that he did, he showed me he was not only with me for the good times but also the bad ones. Yet in my heart, I questioned God's timing:

"But, Lord, a relationship? But, Lord, Tulsa, Oklahoma? Lord, what is going on? Was I crazy or just temporarily insane?"

George faithfully continued to visit me in Dallas on the weekends and I flew to Tulsa for lunch occasionally. It was less than three months after George and I first met when I realized our relationship had become more than casual. This scared me. I was still gun-shy. So I sat down and attempted to put my thoughts, feelings, and prayers concerning George down on paper. I wrote:

Only two months ago I felt so safe and secure, totally in control of my life . . . and lonely. Only weeks ago I told Carmen I didn't want to ever fall in love again. It is painful and draining. I said I would rather win the sweepstakes and be totally self-sufficient. That way I would never be hurt by a man again.

Now, a man has walked into my life, and in a very short time he has begun to redefine my hopes and dreams. Can I dare risk the thought of such hopes?

Why would I allow myself to consider a relationship? George did not possess money, power, or position—the things my carnal nature admired in a man. So where did the attraction come from?

Since the first day we met I felt drawn to him. George exuded a peace that soothed me and gave me a joy that lifted my spirit. Not to mention, he is a perfect physical specimen—tall, dark, handsome, and wise. Lord, You surely did good when You molded this one. George appears to be as appealing from the inside out as he does from the outside in. He seems to be secure with who he is and what he wants out of life. But he is not cocky or boastful. George possesses a wonderful sense of humor. He makes me laugh, which is very comforting to me. Too often I take life much too seriously.

We both share a sense of boldness and honesty in facing this relationship. I have never felt this good, this soon, about a potential mate. Is this because of the honesty and boldness, or is it timing? Or could it be that our spirits are in agreement? Is it because neither of us is expecting perfection, but acceptance, for who we are? Or is it all of these and more?

First and foremost, I need to know God's hand is on this relationship. The reason I believe it is is because I am at peace with this man like I have never been before. But I am also at peace with myself more than I have ever been before. I think we could learn to nurture each other. We both seem to be open to learn. I think we could be good for each other.

Why am I so scared? I feel safe here in my home in Irving, Texas. I've gone through so much here. My life is steady and consistent . . . and lonely. Why do I feel like I am walking the plank of a wayward ship, feeling as though I'm about to enter the vastness of the open sea with its dangers and excitement and beauty, but still, the unknown.

Will I be swallowed up by a whale that carries me to safety and a life of happily ever after? Or will I be eaten by the sharks, or even worse, only half eaten so that I'm still miserable and only able to wish on death so I can be at peace once more?

God said, "perfect love drives out fear" (1 John 4:18).God said, "Never will I leave you; never will I forsake you." So we say with confidence, "The Lord is my helper; I will not be afraid. What can man do to me?" (Heb. 13:5–6).

Faith! If I keep my eyes focused on the Lord and constantly attempt to please Him above all else in my life, I will not have to worry about all the worldly disasters that could come my way. God promises all things are possible to the believer. "Everything is possible for him who believes" (Mark 9:23). God also says, "if you believe, you will receive whatever you ask for in prayer" (Matt. 21:22).

O Lord, give me the patience not to expect a perfect relationship. Fill me with hope that with Your help and our efforts we will be a relationship pleasing to your eyes. Allow me to be wise to your wishes. You know my desire for a mate is for one of Your choosing and not mine. If for some reason this relationship is not Your will, let the separation be a gentle one.

I felt a peace come over me in the days to follow. My fear of being involved in a close relationship was gone. I handed our relationship over to God. If it was to be, I knew it was a blessing from Him. If I lost my inner peace, I knew it was not from God. If this man honored God, me, and my daughter, I would accept this relationship as yet another blessing from a merciful, loving Father.

TRIED AND TESTED

George and I hit a major glitch in our relationship on one of my visits to Tulsa. We had engaged in a long, in-depth conversation concerning the role of a man and a woman in a marriage commitment. George viewed marriage as an equal partnership. He saw it resembling a merger of sorts. I tried to explain the church's view of a man's role as the head of the household. And where we would be partners of a sort, the man held the position of authority as well as the responsibilities that went with that authority. George disagreed with that position. Then he went on to say he wasn't really enthused about further spiritual growth right now. I couldn't believe my ears!

"Are you saved?" I blurted out.

"I'd like to think so. I'm a pretty nice guy, and I try to stay out of trouble."

"You don't know for sure if you are going to heaven, and you're not interested in spiritual growth right now?"

"Who really knows if you're saved for sure?"

"I do! And it has nothing to do with being a nice person. It has to do with accepting Jesus Christ as your Lord and Savior. It's clinging to your faith as the most valuable commodity there is."

"I understand your position, Deborah. You've been through a lot in your life. I'm sure faith was a great comfort to you in your time of need."

"No, George! I'm afraid you clearly don't understand my position at all. And as much as I'd love to make it all clear to you, for your own sake, I'm emotionally unable to deal with that right now. Would you please take me to the airport?"

"Right now?"

"Yes! I'll pack up Felicia if you will call and check on the next flight to Dallas."

He looked at me in disbelief, but when he saw me packing my things, he went to make the call. Was I over-reacting? I was too hurt to think rationally. I needed some time and distance to sort things out.

Very little was said on the way to the airport, but I had to make my position clear before I left. I stared straight ahead so as not to be distracted as I attempted to explain myself.

"George, my whole way of life is centered around my relationship with God and His Son Jesus Christ. My faith is not a hobby or an extracurricular activity. It's a passion! Where many issues in life are up for interpretation, God's Word is not.

I'm not saying that you are not good enough for me because you are not where I am spiritually. But I must be assured that you are willing to grow into what God has planned for you in order to continue our relationship. Without that assurance, I cannot see you again," I said with tears running down my face.

"I'm sorry. I wish I could say what you wanted to

hear Deborah, but I can't. I would be lying if I did. I'm just not sure where I stand in my spiritual commitment."

"I greatly appreciate your honesty. Please don't say anything that you are not ready to say. But please respect my position. This is not by any means an ultimatum."

"I understand," he said as he pulled into the airport.

"Please just drop us off in front."

"I'd really like to help you to the gate."

"No, please, it will be better this way. I need some time to gather my thoughts."

"OK, if you're sure."

"I'm sure."

I no sooner cleared his line of vision when the tears raced uncontrollably down my face. Fortunately the airport was not a strange place for tears. Once I was settled on the plane and Felicia was asleep in my lap, I tried to erase all my dreams of a happily-ever-after with George. This must not have been God's plan for my life. It wasn't long before I felt a divine peace come over me. I didn't ask God why. I had a strange reassurance that everything would work out fine.

I recalled the story in the Old Testament when God asked Abraham to sacrifice his only son in order to test his love. Was this my test? I was not about to question God, and I was so thankful that I served a faithful God who I knew would look out for my best interest as long as I put my trust in Him.

When I got home I boxed up all pictures of George and anything else he had given me or Felicia. I didn't want to be reminded about what might have been. I needed to move forward.

Five days later, George's sister Suzanne called me and asked me to lunch. I told her George and I weren't seeing each other anymore. She said she knew that but she really wanted to talk to me. We shared a nice lunch, and I explained my position. She completely understood. She told me she had been praying for several years for George to make a recommitment to God. She hoped I would be the incentive but not the motive behind his decision.

Nine days after I left George in Tulsa, he called.

"Deborah, I've been doing a lot of thinking and if you can be patient with me I think I'd like to learn more about your passion. I'm not saying this to make you happy, but I'm saying this because it will make me happy. It may take some time, but Rome wasn't built in a day."

Within weeks George rededicated his life to God and the "Bonding Agent," the Holy Spirit, was more powerful than super glue.

God continued to bless our relationship. Even though George had many other relationships before me in his more than twenty years of dating, he had not been engaged nor had he lived with another girl. To this day I believe God saved him for me.

A year after the courtship began God said, "This is good, this is right, and now is the time." George and I became engaged to be married. George presented to me a beautiful diamond that he brought back from the African diamond mines for his future bride. George's family lovingly and graciously welcomed Felicia and me into the family.

Once engaged, I was ready to get married right away and get on with our lives. But my wise and patient mate wanted everything to be just right. George wanted to wait until the spring so he could get time off work for an appropriate honeymoon. That meant waiting six months. George didn't care what kind of wedding ceremony we had, but we needed time to prepare mentally and spiritually. We attended premarital counseling classes and planned a lovely small wedding that I cherish to this day.

George was faithful to me and God about keeping our relationship sexually pure. Throughout our engagement it became increasingly harder for me. To George, it became a challenge. He knew how important it was to me, so when I got out of line, he was my rock. And for our faithfulness, God truly blessed our wedding night. We had anointed sex. Wow!

Two weeks after we returned from our honeymoon Felicia turned two years old. George was anxious to start the adoption proceedings for Felicia. Seven months later Felicia's official adoption day was a celebration day for all three of us.

George and I where married in 1987. Even though I had fallen short of God's best for my life, our gracious Father offered me healing, love, a wonderful godly husband. We now have three beautiful, healthy daughters. Why, oh why, would I ever leave Your side, my gracious Father, my Healer, my Counselor, my Friend. What a merciful God we serve!

CHAPTER 10

How to Be a Child of God

The story of mankind began in the Garden of Eden. God created the world and everything in it, and it was perfect. Then He created man to commune with Him, and Adam and Eve were in daily communion with God. They walked and talked together in the cool of the day. Life was peaceful; everything was in perfect order. There were no alarm clocks, no jobs to rush to, no homework, no bills, and no death. There was no need to cry out to God. He was standing right there. God gave Adam and Eve everything because He loved them. Life was good.

God also gave Adam and Eve a free will. They possessed the ability to make choices for their lives; man was a free, moral agent. There was only one condition. God had placed one tree in the center of the garden, the tree of life, and commanded that they not eat of that tree.

But there was also an entity to be dealt with, or they would have no reason to have a free will. That entity was Satan. The Scripture says that he was more subtle than any of the beasts of the field. And he was the first to show up and tempt Adam and Eve. He encouraged them to do the very thing that God had forbidden— eat of the tree of life. And by exercising their free will, they chose to eat of the forbidden fruit. This act is called "The Fall of mankind." It is also called, "the original sin."

THE SEPARATION OF GOD AND MAN

When Adam and Eve exercised their free will and disobeyed God, God had no choice but to separate Himself from sin, and He drove them out of the Garden of Eden.

As descendants of Adam and Eve we all inherited their sinful nature. The Bible says, "For all have sinned and fall short of the glory of God" (Rom. 3:23).

> For the wages of sin is death, but the gift of
> God is eternal life in Christ Jesus our Lord.
> —ROMANS 6:23

There was a big gap between God and man, a gap no man made sacrifice could ever bridge. So God in His infinite mercy sent a remedy. He sent His only Son, in the form of human flesh, to be the sacrifice for my sin and yours, thereby reestablishing perfect communication between God and man. Jesus is the bridge that closes the gap between God and man. "Man responds to God's love by crossing the bridge through trusting Jesus Christ and receiving Him by personal invitation."[13]

The Bible says, "Yet to all who receive him, to those who believed in his name, he gave the right to become children of God" (John 1:12).

For God so loved the world, that he gave his
only begotten Son, that whosoever believeth
in him should not perish, but have ever-
lasting life.

—JOHN 3:16

FORGIVENESS SUPERSEDES FAILURE

If you are already a Christian, but have failed Him,
and you are seeking His forgiveness, you may confess
your sins. The Bible says, "If we confess our sins, he is
faithful and just and will forgive our sins and purify us
from all unrighteousness" (1 John 1:9).

Then I acknowledged my sin to you and did
not cover up my iniquity. I said, "I will confess my transgressions to the Lord"—and
you forgave the guilt of my sin.

—PSALM 32:5

THE CHANGE

Following Christ is not without its costs. It is not
always easy. Repentance requires a change in lifestyle,
because your are now a new person in Christ! But the
rewards are great. God does not leave us in the dark
about what is right and wrong, but in the Bible, He
offers us rules for holy living. He tells us to set our
hearts on things above and not on earthly things.
When you rededicated your life to the Lord and
became born again—you died to yourself, and your
life is now hidden in Jesus. So when God looks at you,
He does not see your sins. He sees you pure and clean,
through the blood of Jesus.
Once you make the commitment to love and serve

the Lord. Be sure and share your tremendous good news with a fellow believer, a minister, or a pastor at your church. When the going gets tough, or you become confused about something, they will be a tremendous help to you.

> Do not model yourselves on the behavior of the world around you, but let your behavior change, modeled by your new mind. This is the only way to discover the will of God and know what is good, what it is that God wants, what is the perfect thing to do.
> —ROMANS 12:2, THE JERUSALEM BIBLE

> Put to death, therefore, whatever belongs to your earthly nature: sexual immorality, impurity, lust, evil desires and greed, which is idolatry. Because of these, the wrath of God is coming. You used to walk in these ways, in the life you once lived. But now you must rid yourselves of all such things as these: anger, rage, malice, slander, and filthy language from your lips. Do not lie to each other, since you have taken off your old self with its practices and have put on the new self, which is being renewed in knowledge in the image of its Creator.
> —COLOSSIANS 3:5–10

THE HOLY SPIRIT

The next step is to pray for the gift of the Holy Spirit. The Holy Spirit is given to teach you gently and slowly. He will help direct your life in the ways that are pleasing to the Lord (John 14).

Know that you cannot keep from sinning by your own power. But if you truly desire to follow the Lord's way, you will be filled with the power of the Holy Spirit to guide you slowly and gently.

Do not anticipate spiritual perfection overnight. If you are a new Christian, or a renewed Christian, remember it takes time to learn how to walk with Jesus. Sometimes you have to crawl before you can walk and then run!

Do not be surprised when you continue to be tempted by sin. You may even fall into sin again and again. The important thing to remember is you can learn to walk with Jesus if you want it with all of your heart. Walking with the Lord, like anything worth learning, takes practice. Your practice begins with studying and believing the Word of God. The pace is set by you. The more you study and believe, the more quickly you learn to walk. Our patient and merciful heavenly Father allows us as many times-out and rest periods as we need. Nowhere else will you find a more lenient Coach.

> Perseverance must finish its work so that you
> may be mature and complete, not lacking
> anything.
> —JAMES 1:4

God knew about our sins before we committed them. My unborn child was not conceived without God's knowledge, "Before I formed you in the womb I knew you" (Jer. 1:5, KJV). Knowing all this, God still chose to die for me and for my baby. This kind of individual and unconditional love exists only in the heart of God.

God is a gracious God and His grace is greater than

the law. No matter what you or I do, God can and will forgive us if only we have faith as the grain of a mustard seed (Matt. 17:20). As I continue to claim God's promises, He has not disappointed me. I pray that you, too, will find such a Savior.

Many years have passed since my child was born, but because of God's mercy and forgiveness, I am able to remember this experience with joy. I was never closer to the Lord than during my pregnancy and the birth of my child. He has never left me. The Lord has blessed my life beyond my expectations.

Now I am attempting to help others who may be hurting. I want to help you. I pray you do not attempt to face this, or any crisis, alone. I pray you will choose to face it with the peace that comes from knowing God's promises. The promises are found in His Word, and are free gifts to each one of us. A gift is a gift only if it is received. Allow yourself to be wooed by the Holy Spirit and receive Him into your life. The promises are yours!

> I will instruct you and teach you in the way you should go; I will counsel you and watch over you.
> —PSALM 32:8

> For it is with your heart that you believe and are justified, and it is with your mouth that you confess and are saved. As the Scripture says, "Anyone who trusts in him will never be put to shame." for, "Everyone who calls on the name of the Lord will be saved."
> —ROMANS 10:10–11, 13

Endnotes

1. The most thorough book I found on the subject is entitled, *Abortion: Questions and Answers* by Dr. and Mrs. J. D. Willke. For more information about abortions and the controversial pill RU 486, see the appendix in the back of the above mentioned book.
2. Biographical notice, Parker Society edition, *The Writings of John Bradford* (1853)
3. Richard E. Behrman, M.D., *The Future of Children*, Vol. 3 #1 (copyright © 1993 by the Center for the Future of Children, The David and Lucile Packard Foundation), p. 126. In the book, *The Future of Children*, by the Packard Foundation it talks about "open adoption."

   "Open adoption refers to the sharing of information and/or contacts between the adoptive and biological parents of an adopted child. There is great variation in open adoption today. Adoptions can be open prior to placement, for a set period of time after placement, or for the duration of the child's life. Biological and adoptive parents are asked to specify at the beginning of the adoptive process how open they wish to be."
4. John Holtzman, *Dating With Integrity* (Word Publishing, 1990), p. 117

Endnotes

5. Carroll Thompson, *The Bruises of Satan*, (Christ For The Nations, Inc., Dallas, TX., 1981, 1984), p. 28
6. Ibid, p. 21
7. Gerald G. Jampolsky, *Love Is Letting Go of Fear*, (published by arrangements with Celestial Arts, Millbrae, CA., 1970), p. 66
8. Carroll Thompson, *The Bruises of Satan*, (Christ For The Nations, Inc., Dallas, TX. 1981, 1984) p. 21
9. Marilyn Hickey, *Break The Generation Curse*, (Marilyn Hickey Ministries, Denver, CO., 1988), p. 11
10. Ibid, p. 16
11. Ibid, p. vi introduction
12. Ibid, p. 11–12
13. Luis Palau, *Going Forward with Jesus Christ*, (Luis Palau Evangelistic Association, 1989)